Praise
How Did I Get Here?

"Could this book be any more intriguing? Wise, self-effacing, sweet, and scorning—to our great privilege, Jesse Browner, on the hallowed path of the classic seeker, rends open his heart and mind. How lucky we are to be invited on his hero's journey!" —Joel Rose, author of
The Blackest Bird and coauthor of *Get Jiro!*

"Literarily informed and philosophically engaged, Browner's essays are infused with a rueful ambivalence as well as an all-too-human longing for possible pasts and futures."
—*Kirkus Reviews*

"Exceptional." —*Library Journal*

"By turns hilarious, profound, and unexpected, *How Did I Get Here?* leaves us to understand that while our lives may have wound up on a different shore than the one we'd set our sights on, that's not such a bad thing. The only possible us is the us who happened."

—Karen Karbo, *Los Angeles Review of Books*

"Jesse Browner's extraordinary inquiry into the path taken is hilarious, moving, and always wonderful. Sometimes baffled, sometimes amused, sometimes horrified, he offers a midway meditation on a life half-lived and clears, for himself and the reader, a new space of hope."

—Joseph O'Neill, author of *Netherland* and *The Dog*

HOW DID I GET HERE?

HOW DID I GET HERE?

Making Peace with the Road Not Taken

A MEMOIR

Jesse Browner

HARPER ● PERENNIAL

NEW YORK ● LONDON ● TORONTO ● SYDNEY ● NEW DELHI ● AUCKLAND

HARPER ● PERENNIAL

A hardcover edition of this book was published in 2015 by HarperCollins Publishers.

HarperCollins books may be purchased for educational, business, or sales promotional use. For information please e-mail the Special Markets Department at SPsales@harpercollins.com.

FIRST HARPER PERENNIAL EDITION PUBLISHED 2016.

Designed by Leah Carlson-Stanisic

The Library of Congress has catalogued the hardcover edition as follows:

Browner, Jesse.
   How did I get here? : making peace with the road not taken / Jesse Browner. — First edition.
      pages cm
   ISBN 978-0-06-227569-1 (hardback)
   1. Browner, Jesse. 2. Authors, American—20th century—Biography.
   3. United Nations—Officials and employees—Biography. I. Title.
   PS3552.R774Z46 2015
   813'.54—dc23
   [B]

                            2014041565

ISBN 978-0-06-227570-7 (pbk.)

16 17 18 19 20   OV/RRD   10 9 8 7 6 5 4 3 2 1

TO NANCY

And you may find yourself living in a shotgun shack

And you may find yourself in another part of the world

And you may find yourself behind the wheel of a large automobile

And you may find yourself in a beautiful house, with a beautiful wife

And you may ask yourself

Well . . . How did I get here?

—Talking Heads, "Once in a Lifetime"

I spent a lot of money on booze, birds, and fast cars. The rest I just squandered.

—George Best

CONTENTS

HOW DID I GET HERE?

Lives of the Civil Servants

We can never know what to want, because,
living only one life, we can neither compare it with our
previous lives nor perfect it in our lives to come.

—Milan Kundera, *The Unbearable Lightness of Being*

If you were on the prowl for a textbook case of the kind of overzealous self-delusion that leads people to make terrible, sometimes crippling decisions, you could hardly do better than to study the professional life and times of A. D. Harvey. For those of us who have ever spent a sleepless night worrying that we may have committed a lapse of judgment that cannot be undone and that we will soon come to regret, possibly with deep bitterness, even a casual consideration of Harvey's stunning career choices will feel like an exercise in hearty self-congratulation. "I may have done some stupid things in my life," we will tell ourselves, "but at least I didn't do *that*." That's certainly how it struck me, probably because I first came across his story at a time when I was deep into an analysis of some of the touchstone decisions that I imagined had derailed my own life.

A. D. Harvey is an independent English academic who has written on British history and literature under his own name and a variety of pseudonyms. In 2013, he was exposed by Eric Naiman, writing in the *Times Literary Supplement*, as the perpetrator of a literary hoax involving an invented meeting between Charles Dickens and Fyodor Dostoevsky in London in 1862. This falsehood had been accepted at face value by a number of his peers and had found its way into the work of several highly respected writers before arousing the suspicions that had prompted Naiman's investigation. But as Naiman dug deeper, he found something more interesting and disturbing than the origins of a minor scandal. What he uncovered was that Harvey's multiple pseudonyms were not merely scrims deployed to conceal the author's true identity; they were actually a shadow community of nonexistent, interrelated academics who all actively commented on each other's work, which they cited in footnotes and monographs, usually but not always in fulsome praise. Because these writers would have been marginal even if they had not been the products of someone's imagination, they were able to operate and publish for decades without detection. Harvey had, essentially, created a minor solar system of academics with himself as their life-giving sun.

Several months after being outed, Harvey sat down for an interview with Stephen Moss of the *Guardian*. The central thing to understand about Harvey is that he is in no way a fake scholar. He holds a BA from Oxford and a PhD from Cambridge and has published a number of books under his own name, with such titles as *English Poetry in a Changing Society (1780—*

1825) and *A Muse of Fire: Literature, Art and War.* By his own lights, he is not an independent scholar but a "rejected scholar." His ambition had always been to pursue a career in mainstream academics, and he had started out promisingly enough. However, for a variety of reasons that are murky, but unmistakably freighted with paranoia, resentment, and grandiosity, he found himself locked out of his chosen path by those whom he came to see as its jealous, unforgiving gatekeepers. He claims to have applied, unsuccessfully, for more than seven hundred academic posts. For the same reason, apparently, he seems to feel that his work is not taken seriously or deemed worthy of attention by his scholarly peers, who do not have the imagination to assess it at its true value. He therefore not only invented his own academic community, with its own highly subjective values, but succeeded beyond his wildest dreams in embarrassing the guardians of culture who had rejected him and in revealing them for the status-conscious, slavish sheep he had always known them to be.

A. D. Harvey is a fascinating study on many levels, but what struck me most poignantly in Moss's article was a rhetorical question that Harvey throws out, almost as an afterthought. "How does the life we live relate to the lives we might have lived or ought to have lived?" I was especially moved by his very literal use of the word "ought." Harvey knows exactly how the life he *ought to have lived* should have gone. This is how he describes it: "Junior research fellowship, a fellowship, marriage, marital breakdown, boredom, frustration, might have gone into politics, might have risen to minister of state, then more boredom and frustration." It's hardly a utopian vision—most people's fantasy lives are not usually burdened by so much failure, ennui, and cynicism—but it is nevertheless what he believes was supposed to have happened to him and didn't. Moss quotes a poem by one of Harvey's avatars, the imaginary Latvian poet Janis Blodnieks, that would seem to confirm this conviction. "I search but cannot find the key / Which will unlock the glowing door / To the life which runs parallel / To the world in which I am trapped." It's not so much that Harvey is living a life that he was not meant to lead; Harvey almost seems to believe that there are two lives occurring simultaneously, parallel yet inaccessible to one another, like train tracks that run side by side for mile after mile, almost touching yet never converging, then diverge in ways that are both predetermined and ineluctable. Harvey appears to be convinced that his parallel life is going on somewhere without him, and he has held on so long in the hope that somehow he can find his way back to it through some sort of switch or portal that connects two worlds that are entirely inaccessible to one another. I am most certainly unqualified to say whether or not this conviction is part of what makes him come across as somewhat unbalanced; it is, however, most surely what has held him back in the "real" world. Instead of moving forward in his own life, he has been trying to break through into a parallel existence that doesn't exist. And who can blame him? He is the goat in the story others have written for him, but the hero in the one he has written for himself. In his parallel existence he is everything that he fears he is not in this one.

In his book *Missing Out: In Praise of the Unlived Life*, the British psychoanalyst Adam Phillips talks about our unlived lives—the "lives we could be leading but for some reason are not"—as the place where we make ourselves feel "special," because it is where we live to our full potential, which is logistically impossible in all but the rarest of real-life circumstances. He writes, "We share our lives with the people we have failed to be," precisely the way A. D. Harvey seems to live in intimate companionship with the highly respected and influential phantom academic who failed to materialize out of an earlier phase of his career. What all our unlived lives have in common is that we are somehow more ourselves, more true to what we believe our true selves to be, in these imagined existences than in our real lives. "In our unlived lives," he says, "we are always more satisfied, far less frustrated versions of ourselves."

One thing you can't fault Harvey for is lack of ambition. He is casually but genuinely persuaded that, had he but stayed on the right track, his success as a mainstream academic historian and/or novelist would have led to a career in government that would have raised him to the highest ranks. Ambition, whether for money, fame, or artistic fulfillment, is by definition always goal-oriented. It is a propulsive desire for achievement or recognition. You can argue about whether it represents a healthy need to excel and test your own limits; a neurotic compulsion to prove that you are more than what you or others may suspect you of being; or, what is most likely, a complex amalgam of the two. But what is certain is that it keeps you moving ever forward toward a perceived goal. Whether you are ambitious for power, wealth, or fame;

to do good in this world or to make your mark at all costs; to prove to a skeptical or disdainful parent, spouse, or community that you can do what they do not believe you are capable of doing, or care whether you do or not; to attain the prizes or amenities of which you felt deprived as a child; to do better for your children than was done for you; to force the world or the culture to acknowledge you whether they want to or not; or simply to make your work the very best it can be, even if no one but you sees the result—no matter what the object of your ambition; it is always in front of you, never behind, and it always beckons you onward, for better or for worse.

There's one memorable line in the otherwise dismal film *Troy*, a supposed retelling of the *Iliad*. Early in the film, as Achilles (played by Brad Pitt) prepares to do battle with an apparently invincible foe, he is approached by a little boy who tells him: "He's the biggest man I've ever seen. I wouldn't want to fight him." Instead of taking the opportunity to teach the boy an important life lesson about courage or righteousness, Achilles fixes him with a sneer of withering scorn and replies: "That's why no one will remember your name." With this line, the ancient Greek quest for glory is ambition boiled down to its very essence—you do it not because it will make you rich or desirable, get you into heaven, or persuade someone to admire, envy, fear, desire, emulate, or respect you. You do it so they will remember your name. Achilles and Hector are still remembered three millennia after their deaths; who among us can hope for the same? Yet if we don't believe in a god, what other afterlife is left to us? "Posterity," says Diderot, "is for the philosopher what the next world is for the man of religion." I myself am so ambitious that I sometimes grow envious reading writers' obituaries in the *New York Times* because I worry that I won't get one as big, or at all; or when another writer's name or work is used in a clue in the daily crossword. Sometimes, if I happen to pick up one of my old books and come across a felicitous bit of prose, I can even grow jealous of myself because I'm no longer the person I was when I wrote it.

But a different sort of problem arises when a very ambitious person, like A. D. Harvey or me, also happens to lead a very active fantasy life, or rather, to spend a great deal of time and energy musing over the parallel life—the road he or she has failed to take. Because ambition is such a powerful vector, if you suspect that you are not living the life you were meant to live, it actually moves you further away from your true goals (those that exist in the parallel life) rather than closer to them. The most cursory glance at Harvey's two lives shows this to be so. Let's interpret the milestones of his self-defined parallel life as a road map of his ambitions: fellowships, marriage, professorships, politics, ministerial post—ambition, love, freedom, fulfillment, and wisdom. He has worked hard for decades, publishing a number of very well received books under his own name, and built a modest yet genuine reputation among his readership. Yet has anything he's done in his "real" life or anything done by his community of imaginary peers contributed in any way toward the achievement of those goals? On the contrary, the harder Harvey has worked the more elusive and distant they have become; the amazing amount of creative energy he has invested in his ghost career has made the possibility of re-creating such achievements in the real world ever more remote. According to Moss's article, Harvey has achieved a certain serenity about his struggles and their outcome, and no longer appears to be oppressed by resentment and ill will. He seems to be happy now in his maturity, or at least philosophically resigned to his strange fate, but there is little doubt that the life he has actually led would have been more fruitful and fulfilling, less bitter, deceptive, quixotic, and wasteful, had he vested less imagination and energy in mapping, navigating, and traveling the road not taken.

The American writer Harold Brodkey suffered from a similar intolerance to the combined effects of ambition and self-delusion. Having convinced himself, and having allowed himself to be convinced by the lavish, unsubstantiated praise of many others, that he was owed pride of place in the canon of twentieth-century literature, he lived for almost three decades on the fantasy that he was writing the indispensable American novel. Speaking with the editor Robert Gottlieb, he was unequivocal in his conviction. "You've published a few good books, Bob," he told him, "but nothing that will make people remember you after you're gone. Now you have the chance to publish Proust—but you must write a check for a million dollars and not ask to see even a single page." During the twenty-seven-year wait for the publication of this first novel, Brodkey was so often equated with Proust (first by Harold Bloom) that he had come to believe it himself and to live out extensions of that parallel life, much as Harvey lived through his avatars. Not even the lukewarm reception of

The Runaway Soul, when it was finally published, could convince him otherwise. While he continued, against all evidence, to believe himself the "voice of the coming age," his career and his contribution are better summed up in Edmund White's charitable characterization of Brodkey as "brilliant but underemployed." Not exactly the kind of legacy anyone, let alone the American Proust, is hoping for.

In Robert Frost's poem "The Road Not Taken," the narrator pauses at a fork in the road, ponders his options, then continues down the path "less traveled by." It is his claim that this decision—to go his own way, rather than take the popular, standard path—has made "all the difference." He did not have any special reason to opt for one over the other, and he concedes that there was probably little to choose between them. He also does not tell us what difference his decision has made, or what aspects of his life have been affected by it. The poem could not be more physical, invested fully and sensually in the material world, yet the common reading is that it is entirely metaphorical—it is not a real fork in the road, it is not a real path, it is not a real wood, and the event described in the poem is important not because of what it means to Frost's fictional narrator, but because it is a metaphor for a significant intellectual or ethical crossroads in Frost's own life.

We all think we know what the poet is getting at. To put it coarsely, he seems to be saying that at some point in his life he made a conscious decision to follow his own star, and not to live according to the way most people live and believe life should be led. By going his own way, he either changed his destiny or embraced it, but either way the decision profoundly affected the course of his life and, presumably, his prospects for happiness, fulfillment, and successful self-expression. Frost never suggests that the narrator is the poet. The narrator could be speaking from the bottom of a ditch, or from jail, or from the poorhouse, or from the grave, for all we know. Has the outcome been positive or negative? Is he satisfied with the result or has it had unfortunate and unanticipated repercussions? Was there a good reason that most people—including those who may have been better informed about the conditions up ahead—took the other path? Does he feel that he made the right choice, or is it possible that taking the road less traveled was a big mistake? Frost doesn't say, and there is not one word in the poem that can be reasonably interpreted to tip the balance in favor of a positive or negative outcome, except for the fact that the narrator appears to have survived the aftermath of his decision. And even that is only implied.

Nevertheless, I'd be willing to bet that the vast majority of readers assume that he's saying that he chose wisely, and that the "difference" was all for the good. Such readers believe that the "I" in the poem is Frost himself, the most beloved poet of the American twentieth century—rather than some anonymous third party, like the unnamed narrator of a novel—and that he would not have become any of the things we have come to know and love him for had he taken the other road. For Frost, we assume, having taken the road less traveled means having taken the leap of faith required of anyone who would choose to lead the uncertain and penurious life of a poet. We do not know what kind of life he would have led had he opted for the well-trodden path—that of farming or teaching, for instance, which he actually practiced, or some other profession suited to a man of his class—but we are left satisfied that taking the road less traveled was the right choice for Frost, and by extension the right choice for all those interested in testing their own mettle, exploring their own individuality, discovering and fulfilling their own potential, and striding onward toward an eventual encounter with destiny. We share with Frost, or we want to *think* we share with Frost, the warm halo of vindication, which, at least for the duration of the poem and its afterglow, is ours to wear because we have forgotten ourselves and have come to believe that we were at his side and whispering in his ear when he took the fateful decision. And what advice did we give Robert Frost, standing there at his shoulder in the quiet wood as he paused to consider his fate? "Take the road less traveled," we told him. "That's what I would do."

And yet the vast majority of us do nothing of the sort. We forget that Frost named his poem not after the fate he chose, but after the one he did not choose. He's thinking not about the road less traveled by, but about the road more traveled by—the road *not* taken. He is not congratulating himself at all; on the contrary, he's wondering anxiously whether he has made a mistake, whether he will one day come to regret, "with a sigh," the choice he has made.

For most of us, the road not taken *is* the road less traveled. We do not strike out on our own but prefer the path worn smooth by the multitudes that have trod it before us.

We profess to admire those who do as Frost did; we make a cultural fetish of the rugged individual and find ways of convincing ourselves that we bear his stamp, despite ample evidence to the contrary. But so few of us do, in all honesty, that we hardly know what such a way of life would even consist of. Is a cowboy—the very poster boy for American individualism—a chooser of the road less traveled? He works long, weary hours for someone else, does not get to choose his own assignments, has no collective bargaining power, is poorly paid for doing perilous work, and is likely to die young and broke. Other than his material and geographical circumstances, the existential conditions of his life differ little from those of a nineteenth-century factory worker. He is a peon, not a free spirit. Yet we insist on epitomizing him as the very embodiment of freedom—as the man beholden to no one and no thing. What about a professional snowboarder? There are thousands out there, the best of them scrambling for corporate sponsorships, the vast majority trudging daily to the bunny slope for the 11:00 a.m. toddler group class. Mercenaries, politicians, stockbrokers? A handful of high-tech and business innovators can plausibly lay claim to having truly opted for the road less traveled, but there are so few of them that we can hardly hold them up as role models whom we hope to emulate. The fact is that, for almost all of us, this is how the world works—there are safe, proven, time-tested avenues to make our way, get what we need to survive, and pass it on to those we love. Calling ourselves mavericks doesn't make it so.

There is, however, one category of human being for whom the road not taken is not a metaphor but a fixed itinerary, and that is the artist—the writer, the poet, the musician, the composer, the filmmaker, the painter, the potter, the sculptor, the photographer. Every artist who takes the first fateful step down that road does so on her own. She has to prove herself to the world with every word she writes or every stroke of the brush. She has only her courage, her honesty, her perseverance, and her skills to rely on. No matter how many have gone before her, she has no one to show her the way, no one to hold her hand, no one to help her when she stumbles, and no safety net. There is no other vocation in the world in which you start off from the very beginning with a backup profession for the very likely eventuality that you will fail. Most of the time you will have parents who very wisely beg you not to do it, or not to marry someone who does. In most professions, imagination and initiative are tolerated and rewarded so long as they do not exceed the bounds of respectable moderation. For the artist, they are the raw materials necessary just to get started. Most professional artists will endure penury, obscurity, humiliation, and frustration their entire lives, and no one will shed a tear for them. Indeed, there's something a little unseemly about an artist who has not starved, at least a little bit. When the idealistic young adventurer Christopher McCandless strode altogether unprepared into the harsh, unforgiving Alaskan wilderness and died of starvation there, as documented in the book *Into the Wild*, most sensitive readers tempered their sorrow and sympathy for his plight with a wary sense of indignation. How could he do something so patently stupid? I suspect that the world at large reserves a very similar reaction for those who venture into the arts. No sense in shedding a tear—they knew what they were getting into. They got exactly what they deserved.

A couple of years ago, as I eased into my early fifties, thoughts of the road not taken were uppermost in my mind. Turning fifty is an opportunity ripe with a temptation that few can resist, and I did not prove immune. Now that it has become commonplace to hear octogenarians referred to as "young," most of us have done the math and found that fifty is more or less in the exact middle of our adult lives. So we put down whatever we are doing and begin to introspect. That is normal, perhaps even as it should be. But in my case, turning fifty also marked my twentieth year in a job that I never expected to have and that, once I had it, I never expected to keep. The reason that I never expected to keep it was that I was a novelist, and had recognized and accepted myself as a novelist by the time I was fifteen years old. I fully expected one day to be able support myself and any family I might have on the proceeds derived from my work as a novelist—that is, by my novels.

By the time I hit fifty, it was clear that that was not going to happen. I had two teenage daughters on their way to college, and I had at least one mortgage. I was publishing novels, sure enough, but what I earned from them would have been barely enough to support me on my own, in a cabin in the woods, without electricity or plumbing, let alone a family. No surprise, I felt trapped. I blamed the job. I blamed my wife for making me keep the job. I blamed my children for being so expensive to feed. I blamed my dog for needing three walks a day. If I were up in that cabin in the woods, I would have had all the time I needed to write the books I was born to write, and none of the distractions. My books would benefit from the additional attention I would be able to focus on them, and they would sell better, and I would be better known. I would be *living the life I ought to be living*—the life I had pictured for myself when I first set out to make my mark in the real world. People would remember my name.

This moment of introspection might have come and gone, as it does for so many people, without leaving much of a scar. After all, people suffer midlife crises all the time without emerging new and improved. That is what ought to have happened to me. Like Rainer Maria Rilke's panther, the image of myself as a caged beast might have imprinted itself in my psyche, plunged into my heart, and disappeared. I was an artist, but I was also a responsible family man who was determined, after a dodgy childhood in an unstable home, to get it right, for the sake of my children, my marriage, and my self-esteem. I did not want my emotional life reduced to what Rilke identified as mere *Verhängnis*—the doom of distraction, anything that stood in the way of his work or prevented him from seeing his path clearly, most especially love entanglements of any kind. I could not aspire, like him, to sacrifice all personal happiness to my work, or allow myself as he did to take ruthless emotional advantage of those who loved him. I was going to make up for all the insecurity that had plagued my own childhood by making sure that my family and my responsibility for it were more than mere distractions.

After all, when all was said and done, I still had it pretty good. I had sucked it up for twenty years and would continue to suck it up, and I would save my best self, and my most passionate ambitions, and my intimate goals, for the privacy of my parallel life. I would reach for the low-hanging fruit, as I ought to have done from the start, and find happiness there. I had to face it—I was never going to be Achilles. Instead of reaching for the stars, I would have to settle for the fairy lights reserved for good dads, reliable providers, attentive husbands, and passionate readers. Instead of being remembered and admired by strangers, I would have to learn to be content with being loved by my family and friends.

And then one day I happened to read a magazine article that stopped me in my parallel tracks. An essay by Scott Sherman published in *The Nation* in May 2011, it was an overview of the life and work of British novelist and critic Geoff Dyer, a writer whose work I greatly enjoy. I began to read with gusto, but I was only a paragraph or two into it when I started to feel sick to my stomach.

The essay portrays Dyer as a writer who, against all odds, has succeeded in living out his youthful fantasy of carefree bohemia, unburdened by responsibility or specialization, and has been rewarded with fame, glamour, and the admiration of his peers. Apparently, Dyer had found a way to live as free as a butterfly, and to get paid to do so. Sherman kept pounding on the word "freedom" as if it were a stubborn nail: "Freedom to write what he pleases . . . freedom to ridicule academia, freedom to travel the world." I tried to keep reading, but my head began to ache. What the hell was the matter with me? But as my condition worsened, it slowly began to dawn on me that my distress had been brought on not by anything I'd eaten, but by what I'd been reading. This was confirmed when Sherman quoted Dyer boasting that "as I grew older I came increasingly to feel that my working life should be virtually synonymous with living my life as I wanted." At this point I was forced to set the magazine aside. My cheeks burned; my vision swam. I felt as if I had been called out and publicly slapped in the face. Even though I had never met either Scott Sherman or Geoff Dyer, and I was confident that they knew nothing of me, it was as if they had discovered my darkest secret, the one I could barely admit even to myself, and splashed it with evil intent across the pages of *The Nation*. "Living my life as I wanted . . ." I felt like Roberta Flack as Sherman and Dyer sang my life with their words and killed me softly with their song . . .

Few people, or at least few novelists, set out in life aspiring to a career in the international civil service. I was no exception. At twenty-two, I was safely ensconced on the Lower East Side of Manhattan, living out the full-blown bohemian template in a $180-a-month tenement apartment on East Twelfth Street. I scraped a living together reading manuscripts and screenplays and writing synopses for a talent agency, rarely working more than three or four hours a day. I spent the rest of the daylight hours writing fiction or translating French modernists. I roamed the streets of Alphabet City after midnight with my friends, cadging free drinks and blackened bluefish from the waiters and bartenders we knew in every dive. It was the life I presumed I was born to live, and there was no reason to assume it need ever come to an end.

But then one day I met a guy at a party who did freelance work for the United Nations. He told me they were always looking for new blood, especially young people who spoke a minimum of three of the UN's six official languages (in addition to English and French, I had Russian and a smattering of Spanish). He said the work was interesting and remunerative, and that freelancers were often paid a full day's wage just to wait around for two or three hours for something to happen. A day's work at the United Nations paid more than a whole week reading manuscripts and screenplays. In the fall, when the General Assembly was in plenary session, you worked full-time for about ten weeks, but if you were thrifty you could live on that for the rest of the year. According to this guy, an adjunct professor of French literature, the freelancers were all literary types like me, supporting their alternative lifestyles with the occasional foray into the real world of suits and corporate cafeterias; the UN, if he was to be believed, was lousy with poets and novelists. The Indian novelist Shashi Tharoor was a special assistant to the secretary-general.

It sounded right up my alley. I was able to support myself, barely, as a reader and a literary translator, but my needs were few and it might be nice to have a little spending money in my pocket for a change. I had spent more than half my childhood living in England, and this new source of income would allow me to visit my sisters, who had stayed there, and my friends across the Atlantic. Another plus was that I would be under no obligation. I would be free to come and go as I pleased, to say yes or no to the work as the whim took me. Unlike a United Nations staff member, I would not have to sit for a competitive exam, swear an oath of loyalty to the secretary-general, or undergo a rigorous security background check. It would not really be like taking a job, because I would remain my own man.

I started work in September 1988, just as the assembly went into session. I barely knew what was expected of me, and the learning curve was very steep, but as I became a little more comfortable with the work, I found that all the hype had been true, more or less. While at times there was serious, challenging work to do, and we often worked deep into the evening, at others I could show up at the office, read or write the morning away, and be sent home with a handsome paycheck. I did this very happily for two years as I wrote what would become my first published novel.

In 1990, the United Nations offered the competitive international exam for a staff position in my office. Passing the exam was the only way to become a staff member at the professional level. Thousands of linguists applied from all the over world; their number was winnowed down to about six hundred qualified candidates who were allowed to sit for the exam simultaneously in New York, London, Nairobi, Bangkok, and Santiago de Chile. Because the exam was so expensive to administer, a roster would be drawn up of the top dozen candidates, who would be offered positions in the service as they became available over the years. Only once the roster was depleted would the exam be offered again. As a result, this was the first time it had been given in ten years, and it would probably be the last for many more.

Even though I didn't want a full-time job, there was no reason not to take it. My chances of beating out hundreds of professionally trained linguists were slim; even if I did, I knew from experience that staff members worked no harder than freelancers, and that they were paid their full, handsome salary even when there was no work. They also enjoyed other great benefits—six weeks of paid vacation, plus another week of uncertified sick leave; free language instruction at any accredited institution anywhere in the world; excellent health insurance; a very generous pension package. Qualified staff also received educational and rent subsidies. Plus, you could never be fired—ever. Not that any of those things were particularly interesting to me. I was a novelist, after all, not a civil servant. I wasn't thinking about the future, because my future was already mapped out. What did artists need with pensions and paid vacations? I was so unconcerned about contingency planning and finding a practical alternative career to writing that only a few years earlier I had dropped out of a very generous fellowship at Northwestern University after my first semester. I had a first novel up my sleeve that was going to do for me what *Bright Lights, Big City* had done for Jay McInerney, *Less Than Zero* had done for Brett Easton Ellis, and *Slaves of New York* had done for Tama Janowitz—all published, auspiciously I believed, within two years of my graduation from college. My novel was about a world-weary socialite who discovers a monster living in the forests of the Carpathian Alps and brings it back to New York City, where it becomes a popular cult figure and monologist on the Lower East Side. It was called *Conglomeros*. With a title and a plot like that, how could I lose? Contingency planning was a waste of time; it was insurance for people who didn't believe in themselves, a cowardly escape route for people who weren't truly dedicated to the arts. Alfred Jarry and Jack Kerouac never had contingency plans, and neither would I.

Still, I took the exam. I can't remember what reasons I gave myself for taking it. I probably didn't need to justify the decision to myself, because I gave so little thought to it. Manhattan was an inexhaustible source of cheap, artist-friendly neighborhoods and apartments; you didn't have to work at all if you were willing to live in Brooklyn, which in those days was still somewhere over there, across the river. It was true that I was about to be married (in fact, we had to postpone the honeymoon by three days so I could take the exam), but there was no talk of children in the air, and how expensive could child-rearing be anyway, if some should happen to show up one day? On the other hand, I felt that my bride and her family would be reassured if I had a job—any job—or even if I merely made a few credible gestures toward getting one. I was very fond of my soon-to-be in-laws and did not want to be a cause of concern to them. So I may have sat the exam as a kind of wedding offering—this is the sacrifice I'm prepared to make for your daughter—although I honestly don't recall ever putting it in those terms, certainly not to them and perhaps not even to myself. I took the exam because I could, ultimately, and because taking the exam wasn't the same as accepting a job. And accepting a job wasn't the same as keeping it forever. And even if I did take the exam, and I did pass, and I was offered the job, and I did stay in the job for a number of years, it was a great gig because it was a full-time job with full-time perks but only part-time hours. I had seen enough of my fellow writers struggle in insecure teaching positions that barely provided a living and left them so strung-out with anxiety that it sapped a good deal of their creative energies. A job at the United Nations would not do any of that. I would never take my work home with me, literally or figuratively, because I would not become emotionally involved with it, the way my writer friends became entangled in their teaching gigs. It would free me of all money worries, for the first time since I'd graduated from college, but still give me the time and the emotional distance I needed to do my real work. In a nutshell, it meant the best of both worlds. It meant freedom.

My professional life at the UN began on January 1, 1991. I had been married for about six months and was about to turn thirty. *Conglomeros* was almost finished and I had found an agent willing to represent it. My wife, Judy, and I rented an apartment on the top floor of a slightly dilapidated townhouse in Hell's Kitchen, directly across the street from the Actors Studio on West Forty-Fourth Street. There were prostitutes on the stoop, crack dealers next door, vacant lots all over the West Side, and I was in heaven. I was in love, I was about to become a published author in the city I was born in and adored, and for the first time in years I even had a job. It was, in so many ways that I cannot even begin to count them, a perfectly normal life moving along in a very happy but oth-

erwise also normal manner. And for the most part, almos
twenty-five years later, it still is.

I want to state for the record that my job is no way Dickensian. After twenty years in the international civil service, I still find it daunting, intellectually rewarding, and occasionally even exhilarating. My colleagues are top-tier linguists from all over the world, each with a unique but equally sinewy story to tell, who take justified pride in having conquered a very competitive profession. I count myself lucky to work among them, earning a good living in an environment of tireless intellectual inquiry and international solidarity. Still, according to Scott Sherman, Geoff Dyer spends his days "wandering through Paris with a joint in one hand and a desirable woman in the other; enjoying himself on the beaches of Mexico and Thailand; reading a book on the waterfront of New Orleans; strolling through the Pushkin Museum in search of works by Gauguin; or taking the bus to Franco's 'Valley of the Fallen' near Madrid." And the reason I had felt so ill when I read this was that my gut reaction was "That could have been me! I wanted to wander, and stroll, and enjoy myself, and take buses!" But I hadn't done any of those things. Instead, I had made a choice to live a different way and am now a civil servant with a very happy family and a dog, both of which I am loath to give up.

It is true that I am a civil servant who is about to publish his fifth book; it is also true that Sherman believes that Dyer has spread himself too thin and has written only one "first-rate" book. But I take little satisfaction in any of that, because I am not sure that I have written even one first-rate book, and it

that I might have if I had spent a little more
Paris stoned and sexually depleted, instead
up at 4:00 a.m. every morning to squeeze in two
hours of writing before walking the dog, making breakfast for
my daughters, seeing them to school, and striding briskly off
to the office, where I was recently promoted to chief and keep
a money tree on the bookshelf.

As a way of giving voice to the feelings that had risen to the
surface in response to the piece about Geoff Dyer, I wrote a
long personal essay about the experience, which was eventually published in *Poets & Writers* magazine under the title "Lives
of the Civil Servants." The essay summarized the decision I
made decades ago, my road-not-taken crossroads, and how
my choice had stayed with me, shaped my life and work, and
raised questions about the obligation of the artist to his creative imperative and the meaning of individual fulfillment
that to this day I am unable to answer. It was deeply heartfelt,
written in three days in a burst of earnest self-inquiry and
anguish, in turns plaintive, stoic, and self-deprecating. A few
days after it was published, a reader named Jacqueline Lapi-
dus posted the following message in the comments section of
the online version:

> *Browner's essay is an overview of the life and work of somebody who
> is fortunate enough to have a job that is "intellectually rewarding,"
> a "happy family and a dog," and five books in print—instead of what
> he imagines to be a life of international adventures. I suspect Browner's
> books would be better if he wrote about the life he has and how grateful*

he is to have it. It sure beats the "personal unhappiness, isolation, and loneliness" that some writers believe is a prerequisite to creating great art.

When I first read this, my initial reaction was: "No, no, no, Jacqueline, you've totally misread the entire purpose of the essay!" Actually, my *very* first reaction was: "What do you mean, *my books would be better?*" as I sincerely doubted she had read a single one. I went on, in my head, to point out to Jacqueline that the whole purpose of writing the essay was an attempt to identify the silver lining of my situation, precisely how to turn life's disappointments into opportunities to understand myself and the social, moral, cultural, commercial, and spiritual environments in which I lived. I deliberately began the essay with all my erstwhile complaints, only to reiterate, again and again, how lucky I was. At the same time, I also made a point of stressing the fact that feeling lucky in comparison with other people was hardly a satisfactory vehicle for advancing a personal philosophy. People want to be happy; they don't want to be happier than someone else. If I expressed doubts about the compatibility of a well-rounded life of material and emotional satisfactions with the creative process, it was neither to embrace nor to reject those doubts, but to consider them, and consider them again, and try to determine if they were underwritten by pathology or neurosis. Jacqueline seemed to think that the point of the essay was to whine about how good I had it; on the contrary, it was to take the risk of airing my doubts about the wisdom and profitability of certain decisions I had made in my life. I had deliberately made myself vulnerable by exposing my

petty concerns alongside my ontological ones, in the hope
that this would ring a bell with my readers. Jacqueline did
not seem to appreciate the fact that she had exploited those
same vulnerabilities merely to make the same point I had
made. I also thought, as I read her critique, that there was
nothing "fortunate enough" about having the good things
I had in my life. Luck had had nothing to do with it; I'd
worked very hard for them, and I could write what I damn
well liked about them.

As I said, that was my first reaction. After exhausting myself in imaginary vituperation against Jacqueline, I was re-
luctantly forced to conclude that she had a point. No matter
how I might deny it, or couch it in false positive spin and
the language of inspirational fortitude, there was a definite
strain of self-pity running through the entire project. Jacqueline had seen right through me. I really wasn't sufficiently
grateful for the wonderful gifts that life had brought me, and
I truly didn't know how best to weigh them against sacrifices
that were at best hypothetical. It was even possible that she
was right about her most painful allegation of all—that my
work had suffered not because of the decisions I had made,
but *in spite of them*. Maybe I really would have been a better
writer if I had better grasped and valued the beauty that was
all around me, within arm's length, rather than, like A. D.
Harvey, grope for abstractions of dubious worth that always
seemed to dance, out of reach, in the penumbra that encir-
cled the campfire of the known world. Was I actually interested in making my life better, happier, more productive, and
more loving, or was I merely, as Jacqueline had intimated,

content to show the world what a clever, stoic, cool-handed intellectual I could be in the face of being disappointed, misunderstood, and undervalued? If I were to have any hope of understanding myself and my circumstances, I might find it wise to stop asking "What did I do to deserve this?" and to launch a new, improved inquiry under the rubric "How did I get here?"

Is there a better way for me to lead my life? Have I made a mistake? I did not invent these questions and so cannot be blamed for asking them. In fact, I've done my level best for fifty years to avoid them altogether. They were thrust upon me, as a writer, as they were thrust upon us all, when aristocratic patronage went the way of the Ptolemaic model of the universe. As human beings, we would all appear to be called upon to face them, in the same way that it is impossible to go through life without knowing whether one's belly button is an innie or an outie. We don't even need to ask these questions; they ask themselves when we find ourselves still at the office at 9:00 p.m.; when we're helping our children with their ridiculous homework assignments; when we're sorting out a year's worth of tax-deductible receipts every March; when, flying in the face of everything we hold dear and everything we know to be true and eternal, we find ourselves running for the subway when another will be along in three minutes, or forlornly switching lanes in bumper-to-bumper traffic. When we rest our foreheads gently on our desks, or our spouse's breast, and long for a millennial sleep; or when we lie awake alone at night, trying to figure out where we went wrong, whether there's anything left worth salvaging, and how we can go back in time and do it all again. Could there have been a better way of doing this, we wonder. We know there must have been, and we despise ourselves for being unable to fix it. It makes us feel weak, lazy, undisciplined, fearful. It makes us feel ordinary. And it's fine to feel ordinary once in a while, so long as you don't truly buy into it; it might even be healthy, like a gentle emetic. But there are few revelations as vertiginous and depleting as the sudden suspicion that you are really nothing special at all, and never have been.

Worst of all is the self-pity, when I know that I should wake up every day with a song of gratitude on my lips for all that I have been given, and bless the unearned good fortune that puts healthy food on my plate, keeps my children comfortably sheltered and superbly educated, and persuades my wife to love me despite all my failings, at the negligible cost of making it slightly more inconvenient to sit down and type out my thoughts once a day. Could it be true that, beyond the "to thine own self be true" platitudes, my life as a hardworking salaryman—refracted through the prism of Dyer's international adventures as a witty, chiseled, dimple-chinned, Oxford-educated playboy—may in fact offer some reasonably valuable object lessons?

Most of us are familiar enough with the lives of the artists to understand that between the extremes—Proust's years confined to a cork-lined bedroom, say, or Boethius's imprisonment, at one end; and Kerouac's completion of *On the Road* in three weeks, at the other—lies a vast multitude of viable and less viable alternatives. Famous authors and poets have made livings in all sorts of ways. There are the obvious ones that everybody knows: Wallace Stevens (insurance), Anthony Trollope (postal administration), Franz Kafka (workers' insurance), Louis-Ferdinand Céline (doctor), Henri Rousseau (municipal toll service), Charles Ives (insurance), T. S. Eliot (banking), William Carlos Williams (doctor), Jorge Luis Borges (librarian), Herman Melville (sailor and customs inspector), William Faulkner (postal administration). Robert M. Pirsig wrote the entirety of *Zen and the Art of Motorcycle Maintenance* between 2:00 a.m. and 6:00 a.m. every day before heading off to his job as a computer programmer. The Colombian poet and novelist Álvaro Mutis worked his entire life in PR, advertising, radio, and the oil business, spent fifteen months in a Mexican jail on a false charge, and didn't even begin his great prose masterwork, the Maqroll novels, until he was well into his sixties. Others have made livings as soldiers, diplomats, courtiers, academics, dentists, magazine editors, landed gentry, you name it.

Yet what is the alternative? I am what some, including me, might describe as a B-list novelist. I'm lucky enough to continue to publish, but to date my books have made little money for anyone, especially me. A few of my writer friends make a handsome living from their work; many more are like me, for whom an advance is just enough to pay off the debts accumulated in the course of writing the book; and the vast majority make nothing at all because they remain unpublished for years or even decades before things fall into place. We all need to eat, and many of us have children to feed, house, and clothe. A lot of us teach, but that avenue was cut off for me when I dropped out of grad school after three months. With hard work, one can still patch together a modest income from freelance writing assignments—book reviews, food and travel pieces, translations, grant proposals, celebrity interviews, and whatnot—but that path has become increasingly precarious with the slow but accelerating ossification of the magazine industry. In any case, I know from personal experience that it is a very stressful way to make a living, and any freedom it wins you so you can devote yourself to your own projects is more than counterbalanced by the constant worry of nailing down the next assignment and paying the bills. It is very difficult to focus on your work when you are always stressed about money. And that, I have to remind myself, is one of the reasons I entered the civil service. I rarely take my work home with me, and when I do sit down before dawn to write, my mind is not clouded by any such mundane concerns, and is free to roam. It is an odd but very concrete iteration of freedom, even if one that Geoff Dyer might not recognize.

Still, even after all these years, I remain plagued by the fear that I may have made the wrong choice. Has it damaged or delayed my career? Would it have been wiser of me to set all else aside—perhaps even including the happiness and stability of my family—in pursuit of what I once believed to be a higher truth? Should I have quit my job because it might have made me a better writer, or at least given me the opportunity I have never had to work exclusively and compulsively on something that I had always claimed to be the only thing I had ever wanted?

I'm not yet ready to answer that question. I am, after all, in midcareer. If my next book, or the one after that, were successful enough to allow me to consider leaving the civil service, I suppose I'd be compelled to consider it seriously. But the fact is, I just don't know if I would be a better writer, or a more successful human being, if I had signed up for the Geoff Dyer school, and I never will know. Most of us spend our time making decisions the consequences of which we cannot predict and are helpless to undo. In my case, the potentially positive outcomes of the road not taken are unknown, as they are for everyone. And when you have healthy, happy children and a good marriage, that question is next to impossible to ask anyway, because imagining the alternative means fantasizing about an alternate universe in which they don't exist.

But say you're the kind of person who, unlike me, does not shrink from such a challenge. Say you are brave enough to sit yourself down and ask: "What would I rather have been doing? How would my life and/or my work been better if I had chosen to live otherwise?" Once you've crossed that threshold, you might as well try to posit an answer. Well, you would have spent more time writing, of course. And not only the books, but maybe also the reviews, the essays, the scholarly articles, at which you might have excelled had your life not been an ongoing exercise in triage, from which everything that is not absolutely essential has had to be jettisoned. And even then, you probably would have had more time than you do now for the other things you love, such as cooking, gardening, reading, traveling. Yes, having opened this can of worms, you'd have to acknowledge that having been able to do all this—to do *anything you wanted to do*, without reference to anyone else's comfort or happiness—might have been a sweet way to live, and a lot closer to the ideal of the artist's life that you'd outlined for yourself in the first flush of young adulthood. If you had really gone ahead and done it, your writing would have benefited immensely, because all the love and energy you've spent half a lifetime devoting to your family, your job, repairing the injuries of a difficult childhood— would have been invested in the only thing that matters in this life: *your art*. Think how happy you'd be now, and how good your books would be, if only you'd been more selfish.

Because, let's face it, isn't that what we're really talking about? Most artists' biographies fall short when trying to describe the creative process and the mind of a genius, but rise magisterially to the occasion of detailing every last opportunity seized by our hero to behave badly. Perhaps the vicarious thrill we get from reading these lives lies in the fact that, whereas genius is elusive and beyond the grasp of most of us, we can all imagine ourselves acting transgressively and destructively, selfishly and irresponsibly, at least once, even if we are not in reality prepared to accept the consequences. The failed marriages and discarded children, the drug and alcohol abuse, the multiple mistresses, the dismissive gesture, the egotism, the haughty acceptance of glory as one's due—setting aside the life's work, you could identify him as a great artist by his foibles alone, the exceptions proving the rule. In this reading, the bohemian artist is elevated to the status of romantic hero who has sacrificed himself for a cause that is nobler, higher, and more endur-ing than the bourgeois comforts. We all know, or think we know, that the history of Western culture demonstrates the near-perfect impossibility, especially in the modern age, of being a creative genius without devoting oneself immoder-ately, excessively, self-destructively, to the muse. And if you fail to do so—as my fellow civil servants Kafka and Melville did—the muse will punish you with ignominy, crushing self-doubt, and oblivion in your own lifetime.

Part of me wishes that I could dismiss this as the bull-shit it is, but I have drunk the Kool-Aid. Part of me really does believe that a great artist has to be selfish, or at least more protective of his gift than I have been. Part of me is convinced that, in addition to talent, hard work, tenacity, a thick skin, and conviction, selfishness is an integral attri-bute of greatness, and compromise an insuperable indica-tion of weakness or fear. Part of me wants to acknowledge that, if I had not spent the past twenty years in a demanding day job, I might have brought whatever talent I had to fuller fruition. But the rest of me knows full well and with utter certainty that if I have spent twenty years as a civil servant it is because that is what I must really have wanted to do—surely not exclusively or ideally, but in the balance. I have not always been happy, and have often come close to giving way to bitterness and despair, or been tempted to blame oth-ers for the wrong choices I have made, but every way of life—most especially including the one I did not choose—offers ample opportunity for anger and recrimination. I don't and can't know if my work would have been any better or more interesting; I strongly doubt that I or my family would have been better off. That might not matter to everyone, but it has turned out, twenty years later and to my great surprise, that it matters to me.

Mentor

One of the earliest reliable descriptions of the lives and morals of bohemians is Henri Murger's 1845 novel *Scènes de la vie de bohème*. A lot of people know it as the source of Puccini's opera *La Bohème*, but surprisingly few seem to have actually read it, which is a shame because it's very funny, fast-paced, and instructive. Its stories and characters are based on Murger's experience as a member of the "water drinkers club," a loose band of artists too poor to drink wine. As a result of his youthful penury, Murger suffered ill health all his life and, despite the book's great success, died penniless at the age of thirty-nine, at which point he was treated to a lavish funeral at state expense.

The novel—a series of interconnected scenes and stories—revolves around the adventures and loves of four young artist friends in Paris's Left Bank in the 1840s. For those who are interested in the history and culture of bohemianism, the book has a lot to teach. For those who now practice or once practiced some form of the bohemian lifestyle, and wonder what it all means in the scheme of things, it offers some surprises and some comforting continuities.

The first surprise, for me, was how fully developed and

familiar the bohemian ethos was at such an early date. I had generally tended to think of bohemian Paris as a culture that emerged in the 1880s, maybe, at the time of Toulouse-Lautrec and the cancan, and then grew and morphed into the Montmartre of the Fauves and Moderns—Rousseau, Picasso, Satie, Apollinaire, and the Lapin Agile. But Murger's bohemians, prancing around the Latin Quarter at a time when the Missouri River still marked the American frontier, are fully fledged in every respect. With a few exceptions, they are very much like the young bohemians I knew back in the East Village in the early '80s—artists who lived in voluntary poverty so as to maintain their freedom while they learned to understand themselves and their work, unencumbered by financial responsibilities that would detract from their focus, and disdainful of mainstream tastes and temptations that threatened to stunt the growth of their distinctive individual voices. They were protective of their authenticity and wary of pretenders, especially rich pretenders looking for reflected glory at a safe distance, as well as nonartists who just enjoyed the casual lifestyle. They wandered about Paris always broke, always hungry, always cold, and always thirsty. They played pranks, cadged drinks, cooked up outlandish schemes to make money, threw wild parties, and got evicted from their domiciles with admirable regularity. They were like the Little Rascals in frock coats.

There seem to be three major differences between the bohemians of the 1840s and those of the 1980s. The first is that there were no women. The artists in the book—a painter, a poet, a philosopher, and a musician—are all men in their early twenties. Their girlfriends, Mimi and Musette, while fully dedicated to the bohemian way, are essentially courtesans. They are not judged or condescended to (much) by the men, but they will never be artists or enjoy the status of martyr to the cause that attaches to their male counterparts. Their job is to have fun and then get married, or die trying.

The second is that bohemianism in the 1840s was very dangerous. One reason why it came to represent a kind of authenticity was that it required not only the well-known indifference to social opinion, but also true courage and stamina. The bohemians I knew and lived among all had some sort of possible fallback, usually their parents, and most, like me, had jobs of some sort, but never professions and never related to their art. They were waiters, bartenders, short-order cooks, or, in my case, readers. We never had much money, but unlike our forebears we were highly unlikely to die of consumption or hypothermia for lack of a winter coat. Even the poorest among us lived in apartments that were heated in the winter and had more or less reliable hot and cold running water all year. We all knew someone with free access to tasty, abundant, and nutritious food. None of us, to the best of my recollection, ever had to burn his furniture to keep warm. In the mid-nineteenth century, the very real dangers of living in a society with no social safety net cast a light but palpable shadow of melancholy over all the high jinks, because so many early bohemians died young, poor, and unknown.

The third major difference is that these nineteenth-century bohemians were very and openly ambitious, including for mainstream social recognition and rewards. They believed that they were destined for great things, and living the bohemian life was part of their apprenticeship toward that end. "Before becoming members of the Institute and ratepayers," Schaunard, one of the bohemians, reminds his cohorts, "we have still a great deal of rye bread to eat." For them, the bohemian life had always been a way station with a foreseeable end, and when the time came to move on and up into the social world—when they felt secure enough in their own talents and individual integrity—they did so without regret and with only a little nostalgia. "What will happen if we continue this monotonous and idle vagabondage?" Marcel, another bohemian, asks. "We shall get to thirty, unknown, isolated, disgusted with all things and with ourselves, full of envy towards all those whom we see reach their goal, whatever it may be, and obliged, in order to live, to have recourse to shameful parasitism." Within a year of Mimi's death, all four have left bohemia behind and embarked on glittering careers, with all the respectability, recognition, cachet, and wealth such careers have always had to offer. No matter how true it might have been, no one in my circle would ever have admitted to entertaining such worldly ambitions in 1983.

That first summer after graduating, I lived in a tenement studio on Avenue C that my sister and her husband were kind enough to share with me. Later we found a two-bedroom walk-up on Twelfth Street between First and A, where I lived in a closet on an air shaft, just big enough for a loft bed under which I housed my bike. Unlike the apartments that many of my friends lived in, our bathtub was in the bathroom, not in the kitchen, but the floors were so skewed that a marble, released in one corner of the room, gathered enough downhill momentum to smash an empty beer bottle in the other. Boric acid lined every seam where floor met wall, like a powdered baseboard, to keep the cockroaches at bay. The walls were so thin that people trudging up the stairs and past our front door sounded as if they were in the kitchen. Jonathan Larson's musical *Rent* was set in our immediate neighborhood, including at the Life Café just two blocks away, but ours was not his East Village of vast, echoing lofts and bucolic fire escapes from which to fiddle and watch the city burn. The landlords were not hip black entrepreneurs but fat Dominicans in stained wifebeaters, and they did not come to their tenants looking to strike louche, tasty bargains when the rent was late. We did not complain about our living conditions. On the contrary, they were our stamp of authenticity; anything less sordid would have seemed embarrassing, bourgeois. I paid $180 a month and wrote at a wooden desk salvaged from the abandoned middle school across the street. Not that I did much writing. In the summer it was always hot, loud, and smelly; in the winter the pipes clanked, the windows steamed up, the mice moved indoors, and the neighbors stayed at home watching TV and listening to salsa at top volume. It was always better to be out on the streets.

Graduating from college had meant coming home as much as it had meant beginning my life. New York City was my birthplace, but I hadn't lived there full-time since I was seven years old, and 1983 was a very good year to get started. Going from Bard College to the East Village was like taking the party and moving it from the living room to the backyard.

Almost everyone I knew was going to be an artist of one kind or another. What else would an artist do? Where else would an artist go? Someone had obligingly prepared for us the perfect stomping ground—edgy, cooler than cool, a little scary, and cheap enough for twenty-one-year-olds with little earning potential—and thoughtfully plunked it down at the center of the known world. We moved in like cats cozying up to the fireplace, and with a similar sense of entitlement. Someone had been holding our places for us until we got there.

It's always easy and irresistible to those lucky enough to have led profligate youths to mythologize them. Life was so cheap and simple, you hear them say. The sex was so available, the streets were so alive with possibilities, the conversation was so much more vibrant, there were artists on every corner and in every basement taking unprecedented creative risks as they sought to give expression to the new world taking shape around them. Everything was *real* in those days, they insist—not corporatized, fetishized, monetized, like it is today. In the East Village of the mid-1980s, you could walk into any Ukrainian diner and hear the same complaints from the gray-haired beatniks and forty-year-old hippies bitching about how authentic it all was back in their day, how narcissistic and nihilistic and self-conscious the younger generation had become. Every generation flatters itself that it's the last to know what the world looked like before it was ruined.

We really were and somehow remain convinced that we were the last cohort before the East Village was gentrified beyond recognition, when young people from around the country flocked there not just for the abundant cheap housing within a twenty-minute walk of a hundred bookstores and a thousand impromptu performance spaces, not to mention uptown and its museums, but to be on a scene that made them feel that something was happening somewhere and they could be part of it. The scene was there long before we arrived, true, but you could bend it and rebrand it and give it your name if you were so inclined, and if you weren't it was big and diverse enough to take you in and find you a place. You didn't have to dance all night, or read poetry in coffee shops, or attend performance art happenings in abandoned churches if you didn't want to. Someone, somewhere was always blackening a bluefish to your taste. Still, like colonists throughout history, most of us felt that we had invented and owned the place the minute we planted our flag there, and that it was now ours to do with as we pleased. That is an attitude that comes most naturally to twenty-year-olds.

My first job was as a clerk at a bookstore on Madison in the upper Seventies, a neighborhood now so thoroughly de-cultured that it's almost impossible to imagine that so many independent booksellers could once have thrived there—like trying to imagine the salt marshes and oyster beds that once lined Manhattan's shores. Working in a bookstore might sound like an odd choice for someone who had just completed one of the most expensive educations in the world, and had graduated with a heavy burden of student debt, but it seemed perfectly normal at the time. Bard College was not the sort of institution that encouraged its students in the arts to take account of or anticipate the practical difficulties that await young artists. What made its approach to education so exhilarating while you were a student—the ability of every student to design his own curriculum, the personal attention and one-on-one teaching, the encouragement to take risks, the emphasis on idiosyncratic self-expression over cultural fluency—could be a potential liability once you were out in the real world. Four years at Bard were enough to make you feel so unique, entitled, and talented that it was unnecessary, and a little vulgar, to make any effort to build a career by making contacts, schmoozing, enduring an apprenticeship. The world was just out there waiting for you to show it what you could do, ready to present you with the little gift box of fame, glory, and cachet it had concealed behind its back. As a young writer in the mid-1980s, I had the examples of wildly successful novelists in their early twenties to prove that native genius was its own best agency. It would have seemed a little sordid and grubby to be seen to engage in any activity that smacked of careerism or worldly ambition. Why waste time grinding out commercial copy, or fact-checking at literary journals, or attending writers' colonies, or doing any of the drudge work to which previous generations of writers had been condemned, when all you had to do was party hard enough, and when the time was right humbly offer up your masterpiece to a bedazzled world? So as I worked on my first novel and threw it away, then on my second (also discarded), bookstore clerk was as good a job as any to prove my bona fides as someone who wouldn't need to worry about day jobs for very long. And when the daily uptown commute became tiresome, I landed even better work reviewing books and screenplays for a talent agency, spending my mornings reading in the park or the library, going home to write up my synopses, and found myself free by 2:00 p.m. to do my own work or to roam the streets at my leisure and size up the wealth of my kingdom. I roamed and roamed and roamed.

There were bookstores everywhere, bookstores like the lilies of the field, sprouting from every crack in the sidewalk, not just downtown or uptown but all over town. They were an archipelago, a myriad of tiny atolls in a seething ocean. In those days I still hadn't published any books, so a visit to a bookstore was never ruined by the discovery that they didn't stock my work. I could spend a whole day skulking from bookstore to bookstore and never get more than ten blocks from where I'd started.

There were coffee shops and diners. You didn't think of Hemingway's Paris when you were in them, but they offered all the same services. In a diner like Odessa on Avenue A, on a cold Sunday morning in February, for four dollars you could have a meal of stuffed cabbage or derma that would last you all day. Or on a lovely scented weekday in May, you could sit and write all day in the quiet garden behind Café Orlin for the price of Turkish coffee and a hummus platter. And then late at night when you were staggering home, just three steps down from the sidewalk on First Avenue bought you an old-world espresso and a warm, fig-filled pastry in the shape of a perfect breast, at Di Robertis.

There were the old steam baths on East Tenth Street, no women allowed six days a week, where skinny, middle-class intellectual kids like me could mingle naked in the Russian sauna with fat mobsters and cockroaches the size of kittens, dousing ourselves with buckets of ice water as we talked in hushed undertones about Karen Finley and Jim Jarmusch.

But mostly there were bars. There were bars everywhere, but our bars had to be of a certain sort. Most important, there could be no NYU students, because they were loud-drinking tourists, locust types, and we were quiet-drinking locals who traveled in small groups or on our own. They could not be new bars, with slick young bartenders who worked with both hands at the same time, or with clever, ironic jukeboxes. They could not be too clean or too well lit, and it was best if they were below sidewalk grade, which discouraged the faint of heart from trying their luck. In other words, they had to be as authentic as we knew ourselves to be, even if we were not authentic to them or to anyone else. Mostly, it was the old-time Ukrainian bars like the Blue and Gold, the Old Homestead, or the Verkhovyna that attracted us. They didn't much care for us in those places; many of the regulars were old guys who had been anti-Stalin, pro-Nazi partisans in the war and were later granted asylum in the United States in return for their collaboration. They would sit at the bar all afternoon muttering desolate praise for Hitler in Ukrainian. Not that they cared one way or another, but they were too worn out to make us leave.

It was a pretty small world. All these bars were within ten blocks of each other. Except for going into midtown to pick up my reading assignments I had little reason to leave the neighborhood. There was nothing much happening in Brooklyn in those days that we knew of, although we sometimes took our bikes across the Williamsburg Bridge to ride among the Hasidim. A friend of mine worked in a Mexican restaurant across town on Beach Street in a new neighborhood called Tribeca that was so bleak and empty at night it felt like an abandoned movie set. You could do the rounds, see who was hanging out, play a little pool, drink slowly but steadily. There was always somebody out there doing nothing much, as I was, looking for someone smart to talk and drink with. And if for some reason the pickings were slim on any particular evening, you could be certain that in any case everybody would be meeting up later that night at the Great Jones Café, after the dinner rush.

One of the owners of the Jones was a Bard alum, and at one point or another virtually all of my friends worked there, and when they weren't working they were drinking and talking there. In those days, there were only three things on Great Jones Street: the firehouse, Jean-Michel Basquiat, and the Jones. Things were beginning to change, the early stirrings of gentrification were evident everywhere, but decay was still the dominant motif on Great Jones Street. Just crossing the Bowery was like an exercise in urban warfare, but then you got to the Jones—a tiny little box of heat, light, and chatter on a block where a single footstep would echo for weeks. There was an Elvis bust in the window and a pulse of cigarette smoke, cayenne pepper, and frying catfish when you opened the door. The Jones was the same age we were—born in 1983.

In my memory, it was always midnight and summer at the Jones. It really was (and remains) a very small place, and when you weren't talking with your friends behind the bar or in the kitchen it was easier in the warm weather to take your drinks and conversation out onto the sidewalk. Every night in those years was a mid-August night—a hot, smoky, pungent night spent hanging out on the sidewalk outside the Jones, a cigarette in one hand and a cheap scotch in the other, Basquiat competing with a full moon overhead as he lurched athwart his studio window or stumbled down for a nightcap, breaking up only when whoever was washing dishes that night had finished his shift and it was our turn to lurch and stumble into the night for a last game of pool or a last opportunity to run into some old girlfriend who didn't happen to be sleeping with anyone special at the moment.

One way or another we were young and we were artists, every one of us—every one of us an aristocrat born to that glorious caste, our breeding evident in the way we swaggered down the street, inheritors of an illustrious legacy, perpetuators of a solemn tradition. How well I remember the first time somebody announced, a year or two out of college, that he had applied to law school. At first it was entirely incomprehensible, illogical, surreal, as if he had told us he was going to astronaut school. And then it felt like the kind of treasonous betrayal of class and clan that stings all the more intensely because it is impossible to anticipate. Law school? That was something *they* did, whoever they were.

And who were we? Just who did we think we were? As a matter of fact, we all thought we were geniuses, and a great many of us believed that we were Alfred Jarry. It seemed as if almost everyone I knew in those days was reading Roger Shattuck's *The Banquet Years*, a history of the roots of the French avant-garde in late-nineteenth- and early twentieth-century Paris,

as told through the lives of four iconic artists—the painter
Henri Rousseau, the poet Guillaume Apollinaire, the composer Erik Satie, and the playwright and literary iconoclast
Alfred Jarry. I learned from *The Banquet Years* what an artist was
supposed to be, the way he was supposed to live, and how he
was supposed to create himself. There were other books that
captured some of the same spirit—books like Hemingway's
A Moveable Feast, Robert McAlmon's *Being Geniuses Together*, John
Glassco's *Memoirs of Montparnasse*—but those were mostly by and
about Americans in the 1920s, the writers and artists who
orbited around the black hole of Gertrude Stein and who
were already living out a semimythological version of a lifestyle that had been invented for them wholesale by an earlier
generation. And that certainly wasn't the case with me and my
friends. We knew we were much more free than that; we were
not the slumming tourists of the 1920s but the ur–starving
artists of the 1890s—the ones who built an -ism, not the ones
who lived and partied in it. When we hopped from bar to
bar, we were doing exactly what all those luminaries had done
first in Paris, and it wasn't a dream, it wasn't in a book or
in a movie—it was *our lives*. Shattuck defined bohemianism as
"scorning recognized channels of accomplishment." That
wasn't bad, but it was only a beginning.

And there was something about Jarry that embodied that
essence. Maybe it was because, like us, he was conscious of
living between two moments, when something had ended
but the thing that was to replace it was not yet clear. That's
the way most twenty-year-olds feel about themselves anyway,
whether they aspire to forge the uncreated conscience of their

generation or no, so it was a useful lodestar for our social ambitions. As Shattuck says about the cultural moment of the 1890s, "Only a few people had an inkling of what was happening . . . something pulled hard and long to estab-lish the direction the new century would travel." That's how we felt about our own time, or at least it's what we wanted to believe was happening. Jarry was just a boy, younger even than I was, when he quit high school in provincial Rennes, rode his bicycle to Paris, penniless and friendless, to launch his literary career, and within no time at all was being feted as a genius and published in all the right journals. "He made his literary debut 'like a wild animal entering the ring,' " accord-ing to his friend Madame Rachilde. That's what I wanted to do! It's what we all wanted to do. Like Jarry, we saw ourselves as "artists who ventured far into the realm of pure buffoonery without abandoning their loyalty to artistic creation."

The Ubu emblem, the spiral that turned the usurper's fat belly into both a target and the center of the universe, was ubiquitous. The word "shrit"—the English equivalent of Ubu's iconic "merdre!" with which he had undermined the foundations of an entire civilization—was on everyone's lips. Most of all, Jarry had found a way to make his life and his art a single, ineluctable entity. He was the greatest bo-hemian of them all, living in abject poverty—quite literally on a half floor, with ceilings so low a tall visitor could not stand upright—and turning his entire life into a performance project. "His life and his work united in a single threat to the equilibrium of human nature." We could do that, too, because Jarry and his successors had blazed the trail for us.

Even if you never wrote a word in your life, you were already halfway there if you could drink in public places while engaging in loud, ironic bombast.

The romance of being a young writer, living poor but cheaply at the heart of the world's most vibrant city, was just too strong to resist, and I can't really condemn my youthful self for having succumbed. As John Glassco put it in *Memoirs of Montparnasse*, "I had no commitments except, in a vague way, to remain uncommitted. I had no wife, no job, no ambition, no bank account, no use for large sums of money, no appetite for prestige, and no temptation to acquire any of them." There would have to be something wrong with you if, at the age of twenty, this did not strike you as the epitome of practical wisdom and good sense. Living any other way, much less being seen to work too hard, or to take yourself and your ambitions too earnestly, would have been a serious breach of good taste. "The enclosed stove-heated *terraces* were the best places to sit and pretend to work, for work at this time was for us more a pretense than anything else . . . it was more fun to play at being a writer." We didn't have stove-heated *terraces* on the Lower East Side, but we had plenty of coffee shops where you could be sure to be seen with pen and paper in hand. We were still a good fifteen years from laptops.

There was no reason to imagine that it would, or should, ever end. Why should it, I would have asked myself. Surely it was just as rewarding to live this way at thirty, or forty, or whatever came after that, as it was at twenty. Everything else would take care of itself. I had left college with vague ambitions to attend graduate school, and the momentum of this idea carried me forward without much conviction. I applied to a number of programs and accepted a fellowship in comparative literature at Northwestern, but I was unable to sustain that level of dull grinding for more than four months. I returned to New York, where my roommate and best friend brewed absinthe in the bathtub, and I discovered the work of the French transcendental surrealist poet René Daumal. Roger Shattuck had translated Daumal's novel *A Night of Serious Drinking*, which had become a cult favorite among my literary acquaintances. Once a year, on the anniversary of Daumal's untimely death at the age of thirty-six, we broke out the moonshine absinthe and hosted a raucous all-night reading of *A Night of Serious Drinking*. I had also begun my own translations of Daumal's poetry. I can't remember now whether it was these translations, or the growing reputation of our readings, but one way or another it was my connection to Daumal that first brought me to the attention of the man who was to become my mentor.

His name was David Rattray. He was in his late forties when I first met him, but I think he may have looked older than he was, the result of some heavy living in his youth. In any case, he was younger than I am now. I was living on East Twelfth Street off First Avenue; David lived three or four blocks away, on Avenue A. This was about twenty-seven, twenty-eight years ago.

David was of the venerable Rattray family of Amagansett, which has published the *East Hampton Star* for the past eighty years. He was Phi Betta Kappa at Dartmouth, where he had studied classics, and had gone on to two Fulbrights at the Sorbonne and a Tower fellowship at Harvard. He spoke German, French, Spanish, Italian, Latin, Sanskrit, and ancient Greek. He was, in particular, a distinguished translator of difficult twentieth-century French writers like Antonin Artaud and Roger Gilbert-Lecomte. While still an undergraduate, he had interviewed Ezra Pound for *The Nation*. And yet, for all his accomplishments, the most dramatic passage in his *New York Times* obituary is a typo—a sentence fragment that was clearly intended to be deleted yet somehow made it in. It says simply: "Read Poetry in Cafes."

I used to go to his apartment, which was all white and very bare, to discuss poetry and French literature—or rather, to sit at his feet and listen. He always assumed that I knew what he was talking about, or had read the writers we discussed, but I rarely did. I would pretend to understand him, then rush home and catch up on my delinquency, only to find that at our next session we were talking about something else entirely. Or he would play music for me, medieval liturgical pieces or baroque sonatas on a harpsichord he had built himself. In my memory, he is always dressed in loose-fitting linen pajamas, like yoga clothes, but that can't possibly be true. I also do not remember any time when we simply went out for dinner or socialized together, but surely we must have done some of that, too.

But the way I remember him best of all is the way anybody can see him on YouTube, declaiming his fearless translations of French modernist poetry. Looking every inch the Roman general in his bowl tonsure, his molasses voice trembling with patrician restraint like a thoroughbred in the traces, he declaims Artaud against a black curtain, all cesspool anuses, cornhole punks, and bunghole souls. A naughty smile plays on his lips until the very end, when he ducks his head and a shadow of fear seems to sweep across his face, as if he has just seen, or unleashed, something powerful and merciless.

David was not an obscure person; he had been a fixture on the Lower East Side for decades, and he was widely respected for his scholarship in a field that had been sparsely populated before he made it his own. I didn't "own" him the way you might "own" a favorite coffee shop that no one of your acquaintance has discovered yet. Nor was he my very special, proprietary study, the way Joe Gould was for Joseph Mitchell. In fact, I'm afraid that many of my memories of him may be borrowed or inaccurate, and I've had to solicit mutual friends for some of the most basic details included here. Also, the span of our closest acquaintance was not long—three or four years at most. I do not, out of respect, even presume to call it a friendship. But I loved him. Certainly, if I did not love him romantically, or as personally as he deserved, I worshipped what he represented to me. He was the household god of my bohemia and everything I aspired to be. He had repudiated his Amagansett and Harvard origins and all their comforts for the unencumbered life of the mind, and wore the mantle of ascetic intellectual rigor like a golden shield. He was incorruptible. He Read Poetry in Cafes.

Most important, unlike Jarry, Apollinaire, and Daumal—indeed, unlike Jack Kerouac, James Joyce, or even John Lennon—he was very much alive. And the beautiful thing about him was that he wasn't young, either. His age and his cragginess were evidence that bohemia did not have to end with youth. There is a way, David's life told me, that the romance, the passion, the focus, and the dedication can be sustained. He was exactly what Jarry would have been had he survived his twenties, foresworn the booze, and knuckled down to his life's work. I wanted to be David when I grew up, and I wanted people to love and admire me the way they loved and admired David.

It was almost certainly my pedestalization of David that prevented me from getting to know him better. It's fairly obvious, I think, that we can never know the person we worship, just as we can very rarely worship a person we know well. Instead, we create an avatar of that person and worship it, as we might a character played by an actor rather than the actor herself. In fact, it's hardly a stretch to say that worship is a strategy, howsoever unconscious, for creating distance, as priests of all organized religions have understood for millennia. Once you have worshipped someone, it is essentially impossible to get to know him, because worship by its very nature can devolve only into disillusionment, and never into friendship. It is also true, I think, that worship is a deeply narcissistic form of engagement that empowers and concentrates the ego the way a convex lens can focus an otherwise diffuse ray of light on a single object. When you worship someone, the light you shine on him is too bright to allow you to see him properly, and at best will illuminate only a tiny fraction of his personhood. In other words, in idolizing David, I was probably more interested in exercising and marveling at my idolization muscle than in getting to know him as he was, if that is at all possible. Some people do try to overcome that barrier, against the odds, but I doubt if I was one of them. I very deliberately say "probably" and "doubt" as if I were writing about someone I don't know very well, or don't remember very clearly. This is not an excuse; I was a stupid, self-involved kid, in case that hasn't come through clearly. Whatever the case, the fact is that I remember far more clearly what it felt like to sit at his feet and listen to him talk—orotund, delphic, yet keenly searching—than any particular pearl of wisdom he may have cast my way.

At this point, I would have been out of college for about four or five years. At twenty-six, I had written one novel, a reworking of a book I'd begun in college and was wise (or vain) enough to set aside, at the suggestion of a benevolent editor. I was probably thinking about or just beginning to take notes for the book that would become my first published novel, four years later. I was also working on my first professional translation, a rather tedious book of essays by Jean Cocteau that was nevertheless a source of some pride for me, absent any other major publishing milestones, and was followed in quick succession with translations of collections of love letters by Rainer Maria Rilke and Paul Éluard. These barely qualified as prestige projects, let alone *succès d'estime*, and certainly didn't earn me enough to live on, but I was far too precious and perverse to lower myself to writing for money, which was a slippery slope likely to lead directly to the seventh circle of hackdom. I suppose that if I'd known at the time that Guillaume Apollinaire had made a decent income writing pseudonymous pornography I'd have tried my hand at it, but anything more mainstream would have felt mercenary. Instead, I continued reading books and screenplays for the movie agency, which took me into midtown once or twice a week to pick up my assignments.

I must have mentioned this commute to David, because at some point he suggested that we meet for lunch when I was in his neighborhood. I wasn't sure I knew what he meant by "his" neighborhood, but one day I took him up on his offer and met him in front of the large office building at the address he gave me. It was the headquarters of *Reader's Digest*, and he took me up to the cluttered little cubbyhole of an office where, he informed me, he had worked for the past twenty years. At that age, I was unaware that anyone could do the same anything for twenty years, let alone edit dictionaries and thesauruses for *Reader's Digest*. Let alone my mentor. My mentor worked for *Reader's Digest*!

How can I write what I am going to write next? The very ugly truth is that I was embarrassed for David—by the fact that he had a "real" job that he went to every day, like a normal person. That his bohemian asceticism, I had come to believe, had been revealed as a mere facade, an aesthetic rather than a lifestyle. And I felt betrayed, too, as if he had seduced me into worshipping him under false pretenses. I had been aware that he had a wife and a child somewhere, but that didn't matter to me. All I knew in my childish petulance was that David was no longer, in my eyes, who he had portrayed himself to be. His life was not a monument to self-sacrifice on the altar of the arts. He was just an editor at *Reader's Digest* who read poetry in cafés in his spare time.

It is in the very nature of a mentor that he should one day become obsolete. He wouldn't be a very good mentor if he didn't. I drifted away, met a girl, left the East Village for Hell's Kitchen. Somehow, as can happen in big cities, the move from one neighborhood to another sometimes involves the molting of attitudes and personas, like joining the French Foreign Legion. It may sound cold, but old habits are easiest shed in new environments, and falling in love had sounded the alarm that it was time to get down to work. David and I kept in touch, but it wasn't the same. At the age of fifty-seven, he walked into a lamppost and knew immediately that something was wrong. He was diagnosed with a brain tumor and was dead within a few months. At that point he and I had grown far enough apart that I only learned of his death by happenstance, second- or thirdhand. I sold my first novel that same year. By the time it was published, I had been working in the civil service for more than two years already.

|||||||||||||||||||||||||||||||||||||||||||||

When Odysseus set sail from Ithaca for Troy, he left his palace; the royal household; his wife, Penelope; and his son, Telemachus, in the charge of his old friend and adviser, Mentor. We learn almost nothing further about Mentor in the *Odyssey*, but Odysseus's confidence and trust in him are supposed to tell us all we need to know. We never actually see Mentor offering any advice or serving as a role model for Telemachus, yet we take it at face value that his job, in the words of one scholar, was to act as "a father figure, a teacher, a role model, an approachable counselor, a trusted adviser, a challenger, an encourager," and that he faithfully fulfilled the trust placed in him, since "father figure, etc." has essentially been the definition of "mentor" ever since. Except, of course, that Mentor was no mentor.

First of all, if Mentor's duties included teaching Telemachus how to be a leader by example, he failed miserably, prima facie. We don't know what guidance, if any, he has ever offered the boy, but we do know that the royal household is a total shambles, overrun by a horde of belligerent and parasitic suitors who occupy its facilities, drain its resources, and intimidate its residents. If Mentor has taken any steps to mitigate the situation in the decades of Odysseus's absence, they have been conspicuously ineffective. Although caretaking is not necessarily a task naturally associated with the role of mentor, acting as a role model certainly is, and by allowing the suitors to run amok in the household he has been appointed to oversee, Mentor has assuredly failed his mentee. It is very unlikely that anyone, most especially Telemachus, would mistake him for a father figure or an even minimally adequate stand-in for Odysseus. Indeed, Telemachus's repeated failed attempts to restore order in the palace are evidence and echoes of Mentor's incapacity.

Ironically, however, the term "mentor" would seem to derive only partially from the character who bears it as a name. Instead, it is again an avatar—in this case, the goddess Athena who appears to Telemachus in the guise of Mentor—who does the heavy lifting. It is Athena, not Mentor, who gives him the advice and the resolve to stand up to the suitors and leave Ithaca in search of his lost father. Athena in the guise of

Mentor acts as the perfect teacher, adviser, role model, challenger, and encourager of Telemachus that the real Mentor has never been—and most likely, never could have been. Perhaps it is unfair to judge the "real" Mentor too harshly, as he is an old man and Homer never tells us what he has suffered at the hands of the suitors. But one thing is certain—no mere man could have offered Telemachus the kind of farsighted advice or the example of undaunted courage of which Athena was capable. Only the father himself, or a benevolent goddess, could give Telemachus what he needed. It would begin to seem as if the mentor's role can be played *only* by a stand-in—an avatar made supernatural either by the godhead or by the supradimensional magic of memory and desire. In other words, Athena was no closer to being the "real" Mentor than my larger-than-life, mutant vision of David Rattray had been a reflection of the "real" David. A mentee will act on the stimulus not of who the mentor is, but of who he believes he is, or who he needs him to be.

So what, exactly, is this thing we call a "mentor"? Many of us know or have heard about mentoring through corporate or educational programs that promote it as an effective and intimate way to pass down experience, practical wisdom, and counsel to deserving young people looking to find their way in a complex and impersonal business or academic environment. I myself recently returned from a four-day management retreat sponsored by my employer, at which mentoring was discussed and encouraged as a rewarding experience for mentees and mentors alike. I have also mentored college seniors preparing to graduate from my alma mater and hoping to find a niche, and perhaps a leg up, in the worlds of authorship and translation. In this incarnation, the mentor is expected to spend time guiding, advising, and prompting the mentee through an environment with which the mentor has become familiar and at ease. If it is done well—if the mentor and the mentee have good chemistry, and are prepared to commit themselves to the process and to leave themselves open to the possibility of change—the relationship can achieve many of the same results as one that is not structured or artificial. One corporate website opines that "the mentor should challenge the mentee by setting the stage for new ideas, since real learning very rarely happens in a sterile and safe environment," and with only a small stretch of the imagination we can agree that this is basically the service that Athena provided to Telemachus.

But we can also agree that this paradigm of mentorship is not exactly what we are driving at here. I am looking for something much more fundamental to the understanding of the self, to what allows us to attach ourselves to an individual in the belief that he or she somehow represents a desirable future version of ourselves or an embodiment of the embryonic virtues and ambitions we hope or believe ourselves to possess and that require careful husbanding and nurturing if they are to flourish. In that sense, the idea of corporate mentoring equates to the true mentor-mentee relationship in the same relative proportion that the "hospitality industry" equates to the dinner party you host for a group of intimate friends.

On the other hand, the online *Urban Dictionary* defines "mentee"—albeit somewhat tongue-in-cheekily and with the oblivious arrogance of the true wiki—as "A word created sometime during the 20th century by people who were ignorant of the word protégé." That is absolutely untrue. "Protégé"—meaning "one who is under protection"—has all sorts of implications about private interests and investments, about advancement and preferment, that are absent from the definition of "mentee" or at least from our innate sense of what it should mean. There is a whiff of self-serving and careerism in the protégé-protector relationship that the mentor and mentee do not share.

So what are the qualifying criteria for mentorship? First of all, to be inspired by someone's life or work is not the same as being mentored by that person. There must be a direct, one-on-one, and intimate relationship between mentor and mentee. You can be a teacher to someone from afar or across the ages; you can inspire them by the example of your life or your work, but you cannot be their mentor thereby. A mentor offers personal and personalized advice; he is in a reciprocal relationship, and on an equal footing, with the mentee. That is another way in which their connection differs from those between apprentice and master, or protector and protégé. This is really important. The mentee does not come to the mentor as a supplicant, and the mentor does not offer himself as a figure of authority or power. They are equals because they depend on one another for mutual honesty. If the mentor feels that the mentee is seeking something more than wisdom—some sort of professional advantage, say, or reflected prestige—the relationship is destroyed; likewise if the mentee feels that the mentor is withholding, or judging, or lying. The mentor does not get to choose what to present to the mentee for emulation. He must give all of himself, and the mentee must be convinced that he is doing so. It helps to remember that the mentee always chooses the mentor, and never the mentor the mentee; once chosen, the mentor must either validate that choice in a reciprocal acknowledgment, or decline it, but he cannot initiate it and it cannot be thrust upon him by a third party. That, again, is why Mentor could never be a true mentor to Telemachus.

Once you've defined the rules that govern mentorship, it's easy to name any number of famous mentor-mentee relationships, especially in the literary world, where, because of the discipline required to sustain a single long-term project, let alone a career, lifestyle is often as decisive a factor as technical mastery (the mentor, of course, has no influence over innate talent). James Joyce and Samuel Beckett; Sarah Orne Jewett and Willa Cather; Ezra Pound and T. S. Eliot; Henry James and Edith Wharton; Sherwood Anderson and William Faulkner. These all fit snuggly into the jewel case of mentorship. Socrates was Plato's teacher, but he certainly didn't teach Plato how to write, and he did not have very much to share in the way of "concrete" scientific knowledge. And yet, because there is no difference in his system between learning how to think and learning how to live, Socrates taught Plato how to think and how to live, and that, in the end, is all we finally need to mean by "mentor."

One of the nicest, and truest, commentaries I've read on this subject was made by Jay McInerney about his mentorship

under Raymond Carver. It hits every beat, including one I
haven't gotten to yet but is probably the most important of all.

*Raymond Carver was someone whose work was tremendously inspir-
ing to me. So I felt very fortunate when I had a chance to meet him
in 1980. I was asked to show him around New York City prior to a
reading he was giving at Columbia that fall. Instead, we stayed at my
apartment and talked literature for six hours, and subsequently began a
correspondence. He convinced me that if I really wanted to write fiction
I had to stop hedging my bets with jobs in publishing and journalism and
make a real commitment, and the next year I followed him to Syracuse
University, where he was then teaching in the creative writing program.
If not for that move, I doubt I would be answering these questions today. Carver somehow convinced me to go for it, and convinced me that
I had the right stuff—I'm not sure how he could have guessed that at
the time, on the basis of a few early stories. He was also influential
in convincing me that the only secret to writing was to put in serious
hours every day for years. I'd been under the thrall of a sort of romantic
image of the writer as a genius who effortlessly produces masterpieces
under the influence of a kind of divine madness. Carver convinced me
that writing was 90% perspiration. He used to call me up every day to
see if I had been writing. And I used to hear his typewriter every day,
down the street, clacking away. That was almost as inspiring as anything he said. He also reaffirmed my belief that good stories are made
word by word; he would sit down with my pages and take each sentence
apart, asking me, for instance, why I had used the word earth when
the word dirt would do. I still hear his voice sometimes, chiding me for
sloppy usage.*

See how McInerney goes from being an admiring stranger to an awed acolyte to a (literal) follower to a humble emulator, all in one paragraph? Note, too, that it is McInerney who chooses his mentor, and not vice versa. And even if the lesson he learns about the dominance of hard work over inspiration is hardly original or unique, having received it from someone he trusted and revered made all the difference. Like me, McInerney had been under the thrall of the "romantic image of the writer as a genius," but unlike me, he was in the clutches of a mentor who was able to disabuse him of the fallacy.

And that brings me to what is perhaps the most critical element of the relationship between mentor and mentee. At some level, the mentee has to want to *be* the mentor. It is not enough that the mentee accept his teachings; it is not enough that the mentee admire his example; it is not even enough, ultimately, that the mentee wishes to follow in the mentor's footsteps. The mentee has to identify so closely with the mentor that, at some point in their relationship—even if it is only briefly—he can see himself living *in* the mentor's life, doing everything the mentor does, thinking the same thoughts as the mentor, and being loved by the same people who love the mentor, including his own self. The mentee has to lose himself in the relationship, willingly relinquish a certain part of his identity, at least temporarily, if the wisdom the mentor has to impart is to be shared completely and enduringly. Look again at Socrates and Plato. We use the word "Platonic" to refer to Plato's works and ideas, yet Plato does not speak in his own voice in the dialogues. He is only a mouthpiece for

Socrates, and other than by triangulating the differences between his portrait of his master and those of Socrates's other students, it is essentially impossible to tease apart what is Socratic thought or personality from what is Platonic. Even if you doubt the authenticity of Plato's so-called Second Letter, in which he asserts that "no writing of Plato exists or will ever exist," there can be no doubt that Plato has deliberately subsumed his own personality into that of Socrates and blurred the intellectual, if not the epistemological, boundaries between the two. In the sense that almost everything we know about Socrates comes down to us through Plato, the mentee has succeeded in becoming the mentor, even if later his own personality and persona will emerge through generations of his (Plato's) own students and followers in the Academy.

The problem arises, of course, when the mentee only partially knows the mentor, or knows the mentor imperfectly, or when forces are at work that prevent the mentee from understanding something critical about the mentor. Mentors and mentees fall out all the time, and it's usually because the mentee has failed or declined to grasp some fundamental, irreconcilable truth about the mentor, or is in fact not following the mentor at all, but the avatar that he, the mentee, has set up in the mentor's stead. Yes, I wanted to *be* David Rattray, but the David Rattray I wanted to be was not David Rattray.

|||||||||||||||||||||||||||||||||||||||||

As I write this, it is exactly twenty years since David's death in 1993. It is also twenty-two years since I joined the civil service—a few years more than David put in at *Reader's Digest*.

Enough distance, perhaps, to begin reconsidering my relationship to David's memory. Maybe I can even, finally, find a way to fire him as my mentor. I owe him that much, at the very least, after having kept his poor avatar guttering like a spent candle all these years.

It was odd that he had never before told me that he had a job. I don't think it can have been on purpose; at least, not in the sense that he would have been trying to maintain some false mystique for the sake of my peace of mind. If anything, it had probably just slipped his mind because it was of so little consequence to him. I can't imagine it would ever have occurred to him to worry that anyone might consider him to be "just" an editor, the way I sometimes worry about being taken for "just" a civil servant. He was doing what he loved to do, and it was all the more precious, not less, because of the everyday sacrifices it required of him. He didn't complain because he had nothing to complain about. Reading poetry in cafés was its own reward. And when I think of him I am ashamed of myself.

That is only one way in which I misread David, or built him up in the image in which I needed to see him. There must have been many others, but of course I'll never know. When I read things about him, it is as if I never knew him at all, which is probably close to the truth and, at the very least, speaks very poorly for the powers of observation of someone who was determined to become a novelist. When I think of the opportunity I had to really plumb the depths of this extraordinary man with whom I was in such close proximity, and the way I squandered it by merely setting him up as a mute statue for my own idolatry, I can only cringe. Read here, for instance, an excerpt from the obituary written by his friend Betsy Sussler:

> David was the most generous of writers, palming his choices in beautiful descriptions as if they were birds: He believed people were gems, precious, and he treated me accordingly. He showered us with gifts: endless stories of escapades, homemade myths and prose homages—all of us would-be lovers—all of us recipients of his devotion. It was returned.

I could never have written that, but I should have been able to. I knew him long enough to get to know him that well, if I had been bothered to. Or take this passage, from the same piece:

> As he was dying, David called each of his friends to say goodbye. "This is David . . . I just wrote the most beautiful poem, the best in my life. Do you know what I'm going to call it? . . . The Debt to Nature. Do you know what that is?" . . . "Yes, David, it's death." "Yes, death, and I am going on a journey, an exciting and incredible adventure. And the thing is, just to go, to let go."

Needless to say at this point, I was not one of those whom David called.

I have never met David's wife or daughter, or any other member of his family, immediate or extended. While he was alive, I did not hang out with his circle of friends, except when we met at his readings, although I have come to know some of them in later years. In fact, almost everything I know about his personal history comes from his book *How I Became One of the Invisible*, compiled and published by his friend Chris Kraus in 1992, shortly before his death. *Invisible* is a collection of diary excerpts, memoir, and critical essays, mostly focusing on the edgy, transgressive twentieth-century French writers with whom he identified closely. Of greatest interest to me is the first part of the book, in which he describes his adventures in the late 1950s and early 1960s on the road and in the underworld with his friend Alden Van Buskirk, a Beat-era poet who died tragically in 1961 of paroxysmal nocturnal hemoglobinuria, a rare blood disorder, at the age of twenty-three. David edited Van Buskirk's only book, *Lami*, which was published posthumously in 1965 with an introduction by Allen Ginsberg.

They meet at Dartmouth as undergraduates who bond over their shared love of classical poetry and skiing. David graduates and travels abroad for several years, and by the time he returns for a visit, Van is a senior, bound for graduate school in Saint Louis. They exchange letters and eventually David, apparently at loose ends, hitches out to Missouri to hang with Van in Saint Louis, where the young poet finds himself socially isolated among the well-heeled graduate community, and gravitates instead toward the underworld of petty criminals, drug users, drag queens, and prostitutes. Together, they cruise the blues bars on the bad side of town, become romantically entangled with a cadre of whores, harvest marijuana illegally grown on public land, and spend a fair amount of time dodging both the police and the pimps and thugs who are naturally suspicious of the young, white, middle-class intellectuals in their midst. At one point, they drive down to

Mexico, where they live in a shack on the beach in Puerto Ángel, take more drugs and befriend new prostitutes, are in turn befriended by the corrupt police chief, and are nearly killed in a moronic attempt at a drug deal. Throughout their adventures, Van's illness grows progressively worse, and finally he leaves for desperate treatment on the West Coast, where he ultimately dies in a hospital in Oakland.

This first half of *How I Became One of the Invisible* hits all the Beat archetypes: doomed poet, drugs, cross-country drives, intellectual Easterners mingling with casual criminals and Negroes in the Midwest, Mexican adventure with crazy junkie police chief and warmhearted whores, near disasters, the nobility of slumming with the "real Americans" out there. David never explicitly references *On the Road*, but the symmetries between the stories of David and Van and Sal and Dean—a starstruck literary wannabe and the object of his veneration, the hardscrabble misfit mystic—are a little hard to ignore. It seems perfectly reasonable when one of their black prostitute friends turns to David to ask: "You boys know what you're doing, or are you just playing?" The implied answer is equally unambiguous—neither of them knows what he's doing, but only David is playing, following half a step behind his idol and taking all his cues from him. David, the double Fulbright scholar, is not yet sure of who he is or where he's going, but Van is. He is dying and he is going to milk his remaining days for all they're worth. To David, Alden Van Buskirk is everything a young artist ought to be: fearless, feral, dizzyingly literate, uncompromising; he must live as if he suffers from a fatal disease. And if he should happen to succumb to that disease in the flower of his youth, his idealized image will be graven in stone. He will be the effigy and the model of the perfect artist—its avatar, in fact—for all time. David's friendship with Van lasted about the same amount of time as his friendship with me, and I was about the same age when we met as Van was when he died. I could never be Van, of course—that role was already filled, and could only be played by the original—but it's interesting to consider that all the time I was busy idealizing and objectifying David, he was busy doing the same thing with his long-dead avatar of perfection.

"A man is disgusted with life and world," he asserts. "He rejects bit by bit everything that his upbringing and education had inculcated." David wrote this about Roger Gilbert-Lecomte, but it could have been about Alden Van Buskirk, Antonin Artaud, or any other poet David deeply admired. Most especially, he could have written it about himself; and in a way, of course, he did—in precisely the same way that I write about myself when I write about David. In an interview published in *Semiotext(e)*, he says: "This injection of irrationality and craziness into the ordered life is what regenerates life in general." The poet's job, he insists, is to "upset the applecart," and finally "to die abandoned and treated like a piece of garbage by people in white coats who are no more civilized or conscientious than the garbage, the sanitation workers." Why would this eerie, paranoid vision be part of the applecart? All the poets David most admired died horribly: Van of PNH, alone in a hospital; Artaud of colorectal cancer, psychotic and alone in a psychiatric clinic; Gilbert-Lecomte of an infection brought on by a dirty hypodermic needle. It seems that you could not be a healthy, functioning member of society and be the kind of poet David admired. David openly acknowledged his own attraction to the darker, self-destructive side of the creative bargain:

> *Maybe I did end up in a black hole of sorts from identifying with Artaud in ways that I had no business doing . . . Within him it was this sense of displacement, of not being your own person in your own skin, of not belonging where you were. And of course I was a drug addict and an alcoholic too, which didn't help matters.*

The difference, of course, was that unlike his heroes, David turned his life around. He got clean and sober; he was a clean and sober and serious and dedicated scholar; he had a family, and a child who loved him and whom he took good care of. He had a job at *Reader's Digest*. Like René Daumal, who started off as Gilbert-Lecomte's acolyte but beat his drug habit, outlived his mentor, and became a responsible, hardworking litterateur with a full-time job editing encyclopedias, David outlived Van—he outlived them all—and outpaced their demons.

What is not absolutely certain is whether he entirely approved of himself for having done it. In *How I Became One of the Invisible*, it's Van, not David, who is portrayed as the true poet, the applecart-upsetter, the injector of irrationality; David is the more mild-mannered "professor." "You boys know what you're doing, or are you just playing?" Is it possible that David had a chip on his shoulder about having turned out so healthy, sociable, and productive? That, unlike the literary martyrs he worshipped, he felt he had not sufficiently rejected "everything that his upbringing and education had inculcated?"

Only one page after all the applecart stuff, this is what David has to say about his job at *Reader's Digest*:

> It's a secure job for me. My working conditions are comfortable and the people treat me very well and I enjoy it there . . . Reader's Digest respects my autonomy as a person and my dignity and independence a hell of a lot more than Princeton University or Yale or Harvard would do.

People treat him well? They respect his dignity? Why wouldn't they? "It may seem strange—people turn up their nose at *Reader's Digest*—they don't meddle with me at all!" For someone who had long disdained convention and appearances, David sounds awfully defensive here. People turn up their noses at *Reader's Digest*? That's not a problem that Van or Gilbert-Lecomte would have been familiar with, is it?

In the end, I think, David did not upset enough applecarts to his own liking. And of course, he died surrounded by friends who adored him, not—like his own idols—abandoned and treated like garbage by strangers in white coats. I hope that he came to see this perverse anomaly as a cause for comfort in his final days.

||||||||||||||||||||||||||||||||||||||||

When I was a very young man, I had a vision of what I thought I wanted my life to be and how I would go about making it that way. It was, of course, a hopeful and a maximalist vision—why would a young person entertain any other, lesser vision?—but because I was raised in a particular way, I had no reason to believe that I could not make it so simply by desiring and willing it. I was able to crystallize that vision by modeling it on someone I knew, admired, and hoped to emulate. He was my mentor in the present and myself in the future. But the future didn't happen the way I expected it would, and it turned out that my model for the future me was based on false premises. I had erred not only in my prediction of who I would become, but also in my understanding of who I was. I suppose a lot of people fall short in the self-understanding department, especially when they are young and self-centered and a little drunk on hope, so I won't beat myself up for that. David Rattray had obviously done it, too, and he was a good deal smarter than I will ever be. Perhaps, in some way, it is not only a commonplace mistake, but a necessary one. When you look back and try to reassess your journey, it gives you a place to start. You start by acknowledging that whatever it is you think you once wanted, you were wrong. You wanted something else, and now it's your job to figure out what that is. It is your job to start overturning some of your own applecarts.

It's fairly easy to grasp the concept of reinventing our own past. We hear about it all the time in discussions about suppressed memories, say, or false identifications in court cases. For one reason or another, our recollection of past events does not jibe with our understanding of who we have become, and our minds alter the past to suit our present bias. We don't know much about the way the mind works, but we know enough that such a trick seems perfectly plausible and, in some cases, even desirable. We do it all the time in little ways. We remember what a little jerk so-and-so was, rather than remember how cruel we might have been to her. We remember how much we wanted to stop and help, rather than the fact that we failed to do so. We remember that so-and-so distracted us at the wrong moment, rather than that we were at the wheel when she did. Conversely, if we are crippled or even merely hobbled by guilt, sorrow, anger, remorse, we tend to remember the bad things we did, or to remember the things we did as bad, and to forget all the good. Whatever the particulars of our case, if we have a case, most of us can agree that our memories of the past are subject to continental drift and subsidence, and that when we turn to look back, nothing is quite where we thought we had left it.

What is harder to grasp is the fact that, just as we continually invent and reinvent our past, we also invent and reinvent our future. We set a goal for ourselves, and when we reach the moment when that goal was to have been reached, and it has not been reached, we reinvent the goal. We were going to be a kinder, more generous, more patient, more thoughtful, more mindful parent, child, spouse, boss, human being; we may not now be any of those things, but we have been improved by our efforts—indeed, it was always the journey and never the destination that was the goal. We were going to live happily ever after, but in fact we are happier after the divorce, and so are the children. Our mentor is the template we have invented for our future selves, but when we reach the future we have invented and it is not what we hoped or expected, we reinvent the mentor to match the reality, and thereby reinvent our own future and ourselves.

Like reinventing the past, reinventing our future isn't a bad thing at all—it's normal, sometimes necessary, and usually healthy. It's what allows us to live in a fourth dimension of which we have only the dimmest understanding. It may feel dishonest, or weak, or cowardly to shift the goalposts every time our punt falls short, but when we learn to accept that our future is not ever what we envisioned it to be, but what we make of it upon arrival, we allow ourselves to move forward and accept that there is not one future ahead of us, but multiple futures, just as there is not one past but multiple pasts behind us. In other words, it is not that David Rattray was not who I thought he was, but that it makes absolutely no difference who I thought he was, because I never wanted to be David Rattray at all. What I wanted all along was to become the person I have become, for better and for worse, and the persons I have yet to become.

Zion

When asked for the secret of life, the sculptor Henry Moore had no doubt about what it was: "The secret of life is to have a task, something you devote your entire life to, something you bring everything to, every minute of the day, for your whole life. And the most important thing is—it must be something you cannot possibly do!" This sounds pretty much like what you might expect one of Western civilization's great artists to say, and he is hardly alone. Yeats: "The intellect of man is forced to choose / perfection of the life, or of the work, / And if it take the second must refuse / A heavenly mansion." Rilke: "This above all—ask yourself in the stillest hour of your night: *must* I write? . . . And if this should be affirmative . . . then build your life according to this necessity; your life even unto its most indifferent and slightest hour must be a sign of this urge and a testimony to it." And of course, while Yeats, Rilke, and countless others like them were artists, with their particular slant on the difficult choices life forced them to make, the "task" that Moore referred to is hardly limited to artistic endeavor—it could be any passionate pursuit, from butterfly-hunting to accounting. Athletes do it; scientists do it; politicians do it; scholars do it. Moore was surely referring to his own experience when he sought to define life's central task, but he was also simply pointing out that people are happiest when they focus their talents and ambitions on one great, compelling challenge and spend their lives exploring and perfecting the fruits of their labor. Work hard at something you love, and even if you may never be best you can always be the best you can be. For someone without god, I find this as close to a workable definition of the meaning of life I've ever come across. Sigmund Freud believed that mental health was defined by the ability to love and to work. So do I. The Finnish novelist and illustrator Tove Jansson took as her motto *Laborare et amare*—"work and love"—and I would too if I were in want of a motto and it were not already taken.

But the problem is that, upon closer reading, Henry Moore's advice is not especially practical for most of us, especially the part about doing the impossible. It's a Pavlovian bell designed to make a young person salivate, but it works only on someone with little or no experience of how the world really functions. Even someone like me, who was lucky enough to know exactly what he wanted at a very early age and even luckier to have the education and ambition to make it happen, has found that doing the impossible is a lot harder than it sounds. Even finding something you love and a little time to work at it every day, let alone devoting every minute of the rest of your life to it, can be a challenge for most of us. Dogmatic assertions of overarching truths are usually made by old men, like Moore, who can't fully explain how they did what they have done and will not ever have to do it again.

On the other hand, while there are many writers, artists, and philosophers who have insisted that you must dedicate your entire life to your vocation if you wish to see it to maturity, there are essentially none who claim that it's better to live a life of divided attentions, distractions, and halfhearted stabs at making a little meaning for yourself and others. So we know that Moore must be right, and we may feel a little sheepish confessing that we are not entirely up to the task of total dedication. We know that we will never be offered a second chance to get it right, yet still we long for a slightly shallower slope, a slightly easier route, a somewhat less absolutist taskmaster, because after all we are not Henry Moore or W. B. Yeats or Rainer Maria Rilke. That is not to say we are lesser than them; we may simply prefer to set goals for ourselves that we are not destined to fall short of. Most of us do not feel compelled to undertake the grueling groundwork that is necessary just to find out if we might be geniuses; we just need to be happy.

In a 2013 article for the *Daily Beast*, the critic Andrew Romano argued against the traditional assertion that what set the Beatles apart and made them a unique success were the thousands of hours they spent performing and honing their craft in the seedy bars of Hamburg's Reeperbahn. Instead, he claimed that arrogance—"a kind of foolish, adolescent self-belief; an ignorant, intuitive certainty that your way is the right way—is the root of all great art." Romano's thesis is that while most people entertain a certain level of arrogance as teenagers, most of us begin to reevaluate ourselves more realistically as we move into adulthood—"to find our proper rank in humanity's big talent show," as he puts it—and recalibrate our ambitions accordingly. "And then we stall out and settle down." The Beatles and other artists, he says, don't do that. They remain arrogant until their talents catch up with their inflated perception of themselves. In other words, even though we all feel as teenagers that we have unprecedented emotional insight and a unique contribution to make, only true artists actually do. Although Romano's point is simplistic (and to be fair, I don't think he's aiming at some great higher truth here), he has a point. Very few of us are Henry Moore, or even one Beatle. Far too many of us are convinced at a young age of our own genius and that the world is only waiting for us to leap upon its stage and dazzle it, but very few of us will have the stamina, let alone the talent, to stay the course, to dedicate ourselves every minute of the day to one task, to the detriment of all others. That's a good thing and just as it should be—a necessary winnowing of the grain from the chaff.

The problem is that many of us who are not Beatles seem to have forgotten the part about reassessing ourselves upon entering adulthood. We have agreed neither to stall out nor to settle down. We stand there like a jilted date, tapping our foot and glancing nervously at our watch as we wait for our genius to manifest itself, and at the late hour when most would have given up and gone home, we prefer to wait a while longer yet and to blame our predicament on anything that hurts less than admitting the truth that this relationship was a non-starter from the get-go. We are the people who fall somewhere in between Brahms and your bar mitzvah band, and there are a lot of us—I dare say we constitute some sort of silent majority. When it came to our turn, at age eighteen, to look into the mirror and admit that there was far less to ourselves than we had once imagined, we refused to submit (by Romano's lights, we refused to grow up), and we carried our arrogance with us into our twenties and beyond, where we dragged it around proudly like an atrophied limb, or the way a cat drags its latest kill into the house in the expectation of admiration and praise, as if this bloody mess were a gift. Sadly, that's true of most of us as well—our gifts, it turns out, are little more than bloody messes, whether we care to admit it or not, and the world is not out there waiting for us to slop them across its threshold. But we persist. At twenty, we were all Mozarts and Rimbauds. At thirty, there were a fair number of us who still thought we were the next great thing, and how lucky we were not to have been overexposed at a tender age, like some burned-out wunderkinds we could mention, before our powerful complex of talents and insight could mature and gel. At forty, those of us who remained had already familiarized ourselves with the pantheon of late bloomers, the martyrs whose visions had been so subtle and ahead of their time that they had been forced to toil in obscurity for decades before the world had caught up with them. At fifty, we find ourselves trudging through the empty, frigid wastes like the remnants of Napoleon's Grande Armée retreating from Moscow.

At some point along this itinerary, virtually all of us are compelled to make compromises that our younger, idealistic selves could never have imagined making. Many of us make these compromises without fully understanding that we have done so until much later, when it's realistically too late to reverse course, even if we wanted to. And it's only at that moment of mature understanding—when we stop to listen to the silence beyond our own heavy breathing—that we come to grasp the full weight behind a phrase we have heard all their lives: "You only live once." For those whose guiding light is the search for meaning in our lives—be it through art, work, family, or spiritual beliefs—this moment can be shattering. You only live once, and you can't take it back or do it over. For better and for worse, we all have to live with what we have done to ourselves and with the decisions we make—especially those we may one day be tempted to regret. At some point somewhere at the further edge of the middle of our lives, almost all of us will stop, take that pause, look around in bewilderment, and ask: How did this happen? Was there a better way to do this? How can we know what the best way to lead our lives is, when we are torn between conflicting impulses—between perfection of the life and perfection of the work?

My books do not get an awful lot of coverage in the mainstream literary press, or what is left of it, so I was very pleased, on the publication of my last novel, to get a rave review by Liz Colville in *Bookforum*. I was even more surprised and chuffed to learn that Colville had found more in the book than I had known was there. One conclusion of hers that particularly struck me was the following:

But Wes has figured out that there is no "one right thing" he can do, as
he earlier wished. In fact, there are really no "right" things, but rather,
decent things.

There really are no "right" things, but rather, decent things! It's not such
an earth-shattering moral, after all, but my first reaction
upon reading it was "That's brilliant! Why didn't I think of
that?" As it turns out, I did think of it, but ultimately, in
addition to being a little trite, it is not all that helpful either.
It sounds simple—don't worry about doing the right thing,
because you may never know what the right thing to do is.
But you will always know what the decent thing to do is, and
because it is never wrong to do the decent thing, doing the
decent thing is always the right thing to do.

But honestly, how does that help anyone in any way to understand the meaning of the decisions we have made and have
yet to make? There are all sorts of decent ways to lead a life
that are not necessarily right for us, and all sorts of ways to
make the right decision whose outcome may not always be the
decent thing for others. As one example, you may feel that it is
"decent" of you to have stayed at your job all these years, even
if it has not always been congenial or rewarding, because it
has allowed you to share the financial burden of starting and
raising a family equitably with your spouse. Because you have,
you have been able to afford to stay in the city, or move to the
suburbs, or relocate to California, or live in close proximity to your aging parents, or reside wherever your preferred
home base might be. Presumably, it has allowed you to raise
your children in a safe, healthy environment and send them

to good schools, where the humane, ecumenical, and life-affirming values you practice at home will be reinforced by their like-minded peers. With a bit of luck, it may also have let you indulge in some of the luxuries that can enhance your appreciation of what life on this Earth can be if you allow it—a few expensive items of clothing and jewelry; a vacation in Europe or on the African savanna; a second home in the mountains or near the beach; modest trust funds to help your children get their start in life. Your decision to make this compromise for the sake of your family might also be "decent" in that it has helped you and your spouse establish a solid consensus about how you wish to lead your lives, and it has thereby strengthened your marriage, contributed to your children's sense of security and happiness, provided them with strong, affirmative behavior to model, and ensured the continuity of generations that will give you endless joy and satisfaction in your waning years.

But what is inherently "decent" in any of that? What, exactly, is decent about middle-class comforts and smug certainties? Could we not all have had perfectly happy lives without expensive private schools, a loft in Chelsea, organic chicken from the Union Square Greenmarket three blocks from home? Sure, it's got to be easier growing up in a place where parents and neighbors aren't constantly stressed about money, health issues, safe and adequate schooling, and domestic violence, but mightn't it also be a typically bourgeois prejudice to assume that happiness is possible exclusively in the absence of such challenges? And as for domestic stability, how many unhappy marriages are preserved in aspic until the kids grow up and leave home before being dissolved, as if raising your children in loveless, airless stasis were somehow the healthier, more enlightened alternative? Is it really better for your children to model grim resignation rather than dynamic change? Half the people you know were raised in so-called broken homes, yet you cannot reliably distinguish them, on the basis of their capacity for joy and good parenting, from those raised in an intact nuclear family. There is an almost infinite variety of ways to live decent lives without any of that; if you had chosen one of those, would that have been more right, or more decent?

Well, like everything else, yes and no. In the case of my family, my wife grew up in a small city in southern Africa, and now that she is an American she wants to live nowhere but at the very center of things, so it is distinctly possible that, had I insisted on scraping by on my writer's income and we could not afford to stay in the city, she would have been unhappy living in the suburbs and even more unhappy in the countryside, and her unhappiness may very well have put a strain on our marriage that could have communicated itself to our girls in unforeseen but surely negative ways—ways that I am, regrettably, very familiar with, having grown up in a home that was irremediably broken in several dimensions, and that I am very pleased to have spared my children. So in the balance, having weighed the probable outcomes of several competing options, it is likely, in a very simplistic way, that the way of life I have settled on is in fact the most decent thing I could have done. These things are pretty difficult to quantify, but on the balance it would appear that I may have chosen the better path for me and my family after all. And I did it all for love, which is more than Robert Frost can claim.

Anicius Manlius Severinus Boethius was a Roman of ancient, aristocratic family whose life straddled the end of the empire and the advent of the Dark Ages. He was a child prodigy with the best possible classical education, and later a senator and a consul, a confidant of the Gothic king Theodoric, a distinguished translator of Aristotle. He was happy in marriage and the father of two sons who became joint consuls in 522, when he himself held the most powerful position in government administration. Within a year of that high point, Boethius found himself falsely accused of treason, jailed, and stripped of all his fortune and titles, with death looming over him and his family. Alone in his prison cell in Pavia as he awaited execution, he turned to philosophy.

Most of us, I am determined to believe, would do the same thing. I'd like to imagine that I, too, in Boethius's shoes, would draw on all my emotional, intellectual, moral, and ethical faculties in trying to understand the disaster that had befallen me, somehow learn to accept it, and seek a way to live in my new circumstances without falling prey to bitterness, recrimination, and despair. Clinging to hope in hopeless circumstances is a basic pillar of Western virtue, and we all understand it as something to inherently aspire to, like selflessness on the battlefield or serenity in the face of death. None of us can be certain how we would react, but we all hope, at least, that we have it in us to rise to the occasion. We all of us recognize that making sense of ill fortune and finding our consolation and dignity therein is both the right *and* the decent thing to do. Although his predicament may have been significantly more dire than yours or mine, he, too, ultimately, was trying to figure out how he got there and how to make the most of that part of his life that remained within his capacity to control.

In the book he wrote while awaiting execution, *The Consolation of Philosophy*, Boethius is visited in his cell by the female embodiment of Philosophy, who engages him in a Platonic dialogue in an effort to persuade him to see the errors of his former way of life and the appropriate use of his intellectual and moral faculties to withstand all vagaries of fortune and secure the largest possible share of personal happiness. This, I hope, is what I too have been aiming at, but Boethius's Philosophy is more goal-oriented, hardheaded, and economical than I have been. The first thing she does upon coming to Boethius is to banish the muses from his side, calling them "hysterical sluts." To Philosophy, the arts hold no answer to ontological dilemmas.

In building her thesis, Philosophy makes six arguments. The first is that if you are going to live by the rules of fortune, you have no right to complain when things go against you, because the very nature of fortune is change. Therefore, to escape that wheel, you have to abandon not only fear but hope as well. Want nothing, fear nothing. "If first you rid yourself of hope and fear / You have disarmed the tyrant's wrath."

Her second argument is that if you want to accuse fortune of having stolen from you, you should first tally all that she has given you, and you'll find you still owe her.

In one man's case you will find riches offset by the shame of a hum-
ble birth and in another's noble birth offset by unwelcome publicity on
account of the crippling poverty of his family fortunes. Some men are
blessed with both wealth and noble birth, but are unhappy because they
have no wife. Some are happily married but without children, and hus-
band their money for an heir of alien blood. Some again have been
blessed with children only to weep over their misdeeds. No one finds it
easy to accept the lot Fortune has sent him.

Argument three highlights the puniness and laughable nature of glory. Fame is restricted and fleeting. "Do you really
hold dear that kind of happiness which is destined to pass
away?"

Argument four contends that wealth does not free us from
want, high office or honors do not inspire respect, and power
does not bring happiness or freedom from fear. Nothing that
does not convey its own beauty has any inherent worth. "It is
only when money is transferred to others in the exercise of
liberality and ceases to be possessed that it becomes valuable."

According to argument five, self-sufficiency brings power,
veneration, and acclaim, and therefore the man who is fully
self-sufficient, even if poor and unsung, has more than the
man who has wealth, fame, and glory. That is the sum of happiness. "True and perfect happiness is that which makes a
man self-sufficient, strong, worthy of respect, glorious and
joyful."

The last argument concludes that all things seek the good,
and therefore the end of all things is goodness. "Whoever
deeply searches out the truth / And will not be decoyed down

false by-ways, / Shall turn unto himself his inward gaze, / Shall bring his wandering thoughts in circle home / And teach his heart that what it seeks abroad / It holds in its own treasuries within." What she means here, of course, is that what we are all looking for, whether we know it or not, is how to live good lives, how to be good people, and that we are always drawn in that direction.

Some people may question whether it is truly apposite to compare the predicament of an ancient Roman pagan in a dark, dripping prison cell, awaiting brutal execution for a crime he didn't commit and on a charge that he was never allowed to rebut, with that of a middle-class so-called intellectual in an advanced liberal Western democracy, wondering why he can't be perfectly happy with all that has been given him. Fair enough, but I would argue in return that Boethius himself intended his thesis precisely for people like me—like us, if I may say so. After all, Boethius himself is already cooked, and he knows it—he is not writing to remind himself to thank his lucky stars when he gets out of jail and goes back to his daily routine. He himself is a dead man, yet he is drawing a road map for all those for whom it's not too late to change their lives and seek happiness by doing the right thing, which is the one thing that fortune cannot take away. He's writing for people like us, and doing so for the most part in language we can understand and make use of. When Philosophy tells him, "I can't put up with your dilly-dallying and the dramatization of your care-worn grief-stricken complaints that something is lacking from your happiness," she sounds pretty much exactly like any spouse fed up with her partner's penchant for self-pity and finger-pointing. She is someone I would listen to very carefully if she came to me with advice.

If there is any significant difference between Boethius's problem and ours, other than the obvious, it is that his has emerged at the end of his life, while ours has emerged right smack in the middle. He is looking backward, summarizing a lifetime's worth of experience, wisdom, and error as from a remove, since it all took place in a past from which he is irretrievably exiled, whereas we have to analyze our experience and its lessons even as we acquire them, on a journey that we have not yet completed and do not know how, where, or when will end, and with a sense of skepticism or misgiving about our selves and the reliability of our own understanding. Everything we think we know about who we are and what we have been through is inherently unreliable, so how can we possibly determine what is good and decent, what is the genuine value of the treasuries we hold in our hearts?

||||||||||||||||||||||||||||||||||||||||||||

I first met Abraham Buchman in the fall of 1988, when he was in his mid-seventies. I knew him for almost twenty-five years, until his death in the winter of 2012, one month shy of his hundredth birthday. He appears impossibly youthful when I picture him as he was when we first met. I seem to see him prancing and scampering like a young gazelle, long and loose of limb, and also down on all fours playing peekaboo with the babies. None of that can actually be true, in the literal sense at least; still, if that is how my mind's eye chooses to remember him, there must be some sort of important truth to it.

Abraham and Essie visited the States twice a year in those days, at the Jewish high holy days in the fall and again at Passover in the spring. They came all the way from Cape Town, South Africa, usually on one of the less expensive flights that laid over in Johannesburg or Atlanta. Despite Abraham's six-foot-plus frame, they always flew economy because there would always be better ways to put the money to use—for instance, a few years later when Judy, six months' pregnant, lost her job and they helped us with our mortgage for eighteen months so we wouldn't lose our apartment.

My wife, Judy, is an immigrant, as is every member of her family, broadcast across four continents. In 1978, her parents, David and Hertzie, left Rhodesia (renamed Zimbabwe in 1980) in southern Africa, along with Judy and her sister, Barbara, and Hertzie's parents, Abraham and Essie, and moved to Cape Town to escape the war of independence then being fought against the white minority rule in Rhodesia. But David had grown up in South Africa, and as a medical student had been radicalized against the apartheid regime, so the idea of fleeing one repressive white-ruled African country for another was repugnant to him. Having been compelled to leave most of his savings behind, and to sell his home in Harare for a fraction of its worth to a man in a Mercedes with a suitcase of cash, his plan was to stay in South Africa just long enough to work and save sufficient money to begin a new life in the United States, to which so many white former Rhodesians had fled. He had explained this plan to Abraham and

Essie clearly and repeatedly, and had tried to persuade them to come along, but they refused to believe that their beloved only daughter would stay in America if her parents chose to remain in Africa. By 1988, when it had become evident to them that the family would never return to Cape Town, they were too old to make the move, but still young enough to make the fifteen-thousand-mile round trip twice a year.

They were far from unhappy in Cape Town. They had a lovely, if modest apartment overlooking the restless Atlantic in Sea Point, on the western slope of Signal Hill, where they would walk for miles along the breezy promenade that separates the city from the beach—an activity reserved for whites until the fall of apartheid in 1994, but which they happily shared with their black fellow citizens thereafter. They were both in excellent, even rude good health, living on little more than apples and cottage cheese and, in Abraham's case, a sniff of whiskey every evening. They had an expansive circle of friends, new and old, within the thriving Jewish community of Cape Town, of which Abraham was an active leader. And after all, they were at home in Africa, where they had both lived for more than fifty years.

But still, in Great Neck, the quiet suburban village just beyond the New York City borders where David and Hertzie had settled, Abraham and Essie's comings and goings were always marked by tears. Every arrival was a perennial reminder of the distance they had had to cover to be with their loved ones; every departure, even back then, was fraught with the anxiety that it could be the last. As it happened, the last was still many years in the future, but its shadow was long, especially on those evenings—be they regular Friday-night Shabbat dinners or the annual Passover seder—when Abraham rose to say the blessing in his limpid native Hebrew, which sounded like a mountain stream gurgling over a bed of clean, round pebbles.

Although the extended families of David and his two brothers always came together on the Jewish holidays—often amounting to forty relatives or more spread out over four generations—Abraham invariably stood in as honorary patriarch. The role was titular only to the extent that he was not the sort of man who required or sought deference. Instead, he inspired in all who knew him unalloyed admiration, love, and awe for the humor and humility through which his kindness, gentleness, and ecumenical embrace of life were expressed. When I first met him, I was made to understand that he held certain hard-line conservative political views with respect to Israel, but in all the time I knew him I never once heard him voice such opinions, or if I did they were couched in such conciliatory, tolerant language that I failed to register them. When a right-wing Israeli or American Zionist talks of his love of the Jewish people, it can sometimes sound defensive and aggressive at the same time; when Abraham spoke of his love of Israel, all you ever heard was the love. His accent, too, was an elusive accretion of Eastern European, Israeli, and colonial British tropes, but his deep voice was so moderately modulated, and always so tilted in amazement at the beauty that life had to offer, that politics in his conversation became a function of his pleasure and satisfaction with his own lot, and the fact that his family was so heavily favored with delightful, intelligent, visionary, and handsome children, grandchildren, and great-grandchildren. He even had the kindest words to say about our dog Nola, who is no one's idea of a visionary. And if you listened to him long enough, you could not help but be convinced that he was right about us all.

At some point in the mid-1990s, Judy and I decided that it was time to sit down with Abraham and have him recite his life story into a tape recorder. Of course, we knew the broad outlines and many details, but we wanted to hear him tell it in his own way, not only to flesh out the spare parts but also to see what he prioritized, what parts of his life had meant most to him. And of course, there was a mild sense of urgency with respect to the passage of time and the risk that his story might be lost—and with it an entire bestiary of Old World family daemons—before it could be recorded. There was something else, too—an odd lacuna, right there somewhere in the mid-1930s, in which no one was able (or willing) to explain why he had left Palestine in a great and secret hurry. Since in all these years he had never told even his own daughter, we hardly expected him to spill his guts for our tape deck, but we had hopes, I suppose, that he might inadvertently reveal something. At least I did; I think everyone on his side of the family was grateful not to know his secret, and none had much interest in finding it out. The fact is, in all the years I had known them, they had almost never alluded to it, and certainly would not have agreed to let it be classified as a secret. It was just something that no one really knew much about, and somehow the topic just didn't ever seem to come up.

The recordings Judy and I made, now almost two decades

old, consist of about six hours of monologue amounting to some fifty pages in transcription. I summarize them as follows, with a few quotes to capture Abraham's voice.

> *. . . and my mother's father's name—that's my grandfather—his name was Abraham. And in Russia they call Abraham "Abrasha." And it is customary when a child is born, when a boy is born, the first-born one is named after the mother's father, and that's how I was called by all my friends in my very early days.*

Abraham was born in 1913 in Kiev, at that time still a part of Tsarist Russia. His family did not live in the Jewish ghetto, because his father and uncles were members of the junior chamber of commerce as suppliers and victualers to the army. It hardly made them immune to anti-Semitism, official or otherwise, but it was a modest extra layer of protection. Nevertheless, Abraham made a point of stressing that although Kiev was reputed to be a beautiful city, it was not a safe one for a Jewish boy to wander about in at will, and therefore he never saw very much of it. The anti-Semitism grew so intense in the years leading up to the revolution that the Jews clung to the hope that the Germans would defeat Russia in World War I and introduce a "more liberal way of life" for their persecuted people.

Following the revolution, Kiev became a battlefield that constantly changed hands between reactionary nationalist forces, Tsarist Cossacks, Chechens (according to Abraham), and, of course, communists. The neighborhood where Abraham's family lived, on the periphery of the Podil district and the city proper, grew to be so dangerous that the children were not allowed to leave the house. One day, the familiar cry "The Cossacks are coming!" rang out throughout the neighborhood. The Cossacks and their horses occupied the Buchmans' yard, but Abraham's father saved himself by hiding "between the ceiling and the roof" for several days, inching himself away from the residence and over the stables, where he sustained himself on the oats that the Cossacks had stored overhead for their horses, and quenched his thirst by sucking moisture from the damp hay. When the Cossacks left, the city descended into chaos, and Abraham's father went on the lam for weeks, while the children stayed with their aunt Gola in the Kreschatik district, where, at the age of six or seven, Abraham first met children his own age who knew how to read.

At one point in his reminiscences, Abraham deliberately halted his narrative and retraced his steps to tell two stories from this time of his life, as if they held special meaning for him—as if he were an astronomer expressly focusing his lens across vast regions of empty space on two tiny, insignificant planetoids of little apparent interest to anyone but himself. One involved a time when his mother was hospitalized with scarlet fever, and Abraham and his siblings were living with his "aunty." Every day, his aunty prepared a care package for her sister and gave Abraham change to take the electric tram across town to deliver it. One day, Abraham succumbed to temptation, spent his fare on sweets, and was forced to return on foot to his auntie's, where he arrived hours late and was duly chastised. The other story involved a shopping excursion with his aunty, in the course of which he unwittingly allowed precious rationed food to be stolen from his basket, with similar consequences. It's hard to know why these somewhat generic childhood crimes and punishments remained so vivid for him after so many tumultuous decades. Was it perhaps because, amid all the horrors of daily life as a Jew in Ukraine, clinging to the memory of these forgettable little incidents made him feel that his childhood was not necessarily one long litany of terror and violence? Maybe it helped him remember himself as a kind of naughty, impish Semitic Tom Sawyer, rather than as a helpless, humiliated Jewish starveling whose father had to hide in haylofts and survive on raw oats and dew. Or could it be that such casual delinquency, even in a child of six, was so out of sync with everything he later became and did that he continued, eighty years later, to marvel at the little stranger he once was—someone who could do something without thinking ahead and come to regret it?

The turmoil and pogroms continued under Bolshevik rule into the early 1920s, and many Jews made the decision to leave once and for all. Some, such as Abraham's maternal aunts, made their way through the Baltic ports to England, where Jewish groups arranged and subsidized their transport to the United States. Others, including his paternal aunts and grandmother, went to Palestine. Either option held its risks, since emigration of any kind was tightly restricted and even domestic travel was strictly monitored, but Abraham's father opted to follow his sisters to the Middle East. In 1924, a group of fifty or sixty Jewish emigrants agreed to meet in Odessa by a certain deadline and to charter a boat to Palestine together. Because of the required secrecy and obfuscation, it took Abraham and his family three or four months to cover the three hundred miles between Kiev and Odessa, where at long last they boarded a steamer that conveyed them across the Black Sea and through the Bosporus to the Mediterranean. In Jaffa, they and their clothes were deloused overnight by the British mandatory authorities, and then they were released into the custody of their loved ones.

Just before getting on the train in Kiev to Odessa, father told me, when I asked him "Where are we going?" he said "We are going to Eretz Israel, to the land of Israel." And from then on I realized that . . . we were going home. From then on, in my mind I established the fact that we were going away from a land where it wasn't our home because of the persecutions and the suffering of the Jews, and I carried on, from the day we arrived in Palestine, that this was going to be our home forever. It was definitely an idea that remained in my life till today, and at all times during all the struggles that the Jewish people went through in the land of Israel, where we came not as invaders and not as just settlers, but returning home after over two thousand years of exile.

Abraham's aunt and uncle were already established in a taxi business and a little café in Tel Aviv, a city that had been officially established only fifteen years earlier and had grown from a population of two thousand in 1920 to thirty-four thousand in 1925, thanks in part to deadly riots in neighboring Jaffa that had led to a mass exodus of Jews. After being privately tutored in Hebrew for a few months, Abraham went to school with his four cousins.

I remember the excitement of the young people in those days, the singing that went on and the wish and desire that everything will be peaceful and everything will be so different to the life our people had in Russia in those days. Of course, we were under the protection of the British Mandate, so no wonder that the type of anti-Semitism that we had experienced was no more there.

But Abraham was under no illusion that he had come to a place where the Jews were more welcome than they had been in the old country. Unrest and violence between Arabs and Jews (known as "Moskovies," according to Abraham) continued, sometimes ebbing and sometimes flowing, yet at all times an inexorably rising tide. In 1925, as a twelve-year-old student at the Tel Aviv High School of Commerce, Abraham was electrified by a speech given by the right-wing Zionist Ze'ev Jabotinsky at a "great public meeting where practically all the Jewish people in Tel Aviv wanted to hear him." Abraham's dates get a little wonky at this point in his narrative, but it is true that by 1925 Jabotinsky had already established his Revisionist Party and its militaristic youth movement, Betar, which Abraham joined as a scout. Without going into detail, the essential difference between the left-wing Labor Zionists and the Revisionists was that the former sought accommodation with the Arabs and the British Mandatory Powers, whereas the Revisionists explicitly sought the establishment of a Jewish state and believed that it could be accomplished only by armed force—a stance that eventually split the Jewish self-defense force, Haganah, between those who advocated restraint and those who wanted to take the fight to the aggressor, as they defined him. Jabotinsky was exiled from Palestine by the British in 1930, and the paramilitary Irgun—Ha-Irgun Ha-Tzvai Ha-Leumi be-Eretz Yisrael, "The National Military Organization in the Land of Israel"—was established in 1931. The following paragraph is the closest thing to an explicit political credo I ever heard Abraham utter:

> *I was impressed to a great extent by Jabotinsky's national ideas. I will not dwell on them, as you very well know what his ideas were—the creation of a Jewish state for the Jewish people, to have the possibility for all Jews to return from the oppressed countries of the world and have their own way of life developed in Palestine. At school, while the political situation in the country was deteriorating, where rioting took place every couple of years, the Palestinian authorities and the British government appointed commissions into the reasons for such rioting, how to prevent it, how to create a peaceful relationship between the people in the country, the Palestinians, and those newcomers. Quota systems were introduced. The Jewish people in Palestine and the World Zionist Organization objected very strongly, to no avail. There was also the situation where the Mandatory Power, in our eyes, was too favorable to the Palestinians and taking their part. They felt that they were the citizens, the residents, of the country, although the areas that the Jews had occupied at that time, where they settled, were either the swamp areas or the sands around Tel Aviv.*

Abraham graduated from high school at the age of eighteen, but because of his lack of schooling in Russia he was still a year or two behind his peers, so he took night classes at an institution that he claimed later became Hebrew University, although I suspect he meant Tel Aviv University. His parents owned a grocery shop on Levinsky Street, at the southern edge of town, just off the road to Jaffa and directly abutting a large Arab-owned orange grove. His father wanted him to earn some money before going on to higher studies, and he found a clerical position at a local real estate agency that sold title deeds to the lots being partitioned in the western sand dunes, lots that their Arab owners had little use for but that now constitute the heart of Tel Aviv. Speaking Hebrew, English, and street Arabic, Abraham prospered at the agency, striking a deal with the lawyer who drew up the leases and netting five pounds for every sale.

Eventually, the municipality expressed an interest in buying the orange grove by the Buchmans' shop in order to build the city's central bus station (as Abraham points out, it was too dangerous for Jews to travel by train in those days). The city hired a Sephardic Jew from Jerusalem named Hodes, whose family had been in Palestine for centuries and whose clientele was practically all Arab, to negotiate the deal, because one of his clients, Sheikh Haj Nimr Nabulsi of Nablus, was a part owner of the grove, along with a brother in Damascus and a sister in Tiberias. Hodes hired Abraham to assist him in his capacity as representative of the Tel Aviv municipality.

A couple of weeks later, I went back to Jerusalem and from there we traveled by taxi to Nablus to see this client of his, who was a part owner. For me it was a great experience to see how the rich Arabs lived in a city like Nablus. In those days, no Jews entered places like Hebron or Nablus or other big cities where Arabs lived. But he was known to them. We were greeted very nicely. I was treated with the greatest respect as well. The servants came to ask what we would like to drink and are we comfortable, would we like to rest? Then the chief cook came out and negotiated, so to speak, with the lawyer Hodes what we would like to have for the afternoon meal. It was mostly lamb, and it was my first taste of the Arab food, which was really tops. That is why I developed a liking for shishlik and shawarma and all the other good things that the Arabs used to eat.

The negotiations, which included an eye-opening trip to Damascus, took a year to conclude, and on the final day of signing in Nablus, Hodes and Abraham were almost killed in anti-Jewish riots that had broken out all over country. They barely escaped with their lives out the back door of Sheikh Nabulsi's palace, and Abraham proudly claimed to have been the last Jew in Nablus until 1967, when Israel occupied the West Bank.

In the meantime, Abraham had become a member of the Irgun several years earlier.

I became more and more active in that unit, and less and less active in my studies. I wasn't a political person; I wasn't involved in politics, but my idea as such was that the Jewish people dispersed throughout the world were entitled to that land and entitled to a place on this Earth where they could continue their life as the Jewish people, have their ideas and have their freedom. The ingathering of the exiles from the countries where they were persecuted and driven from place to place

and treated as secondhand citizens, and less than secondhand citizens,
in the best of times—to me that was my political ideology. And to stop
this rioting and to stop the mandatory powers from discontinuing the
immigration to the country, and to stop them from making it impossible
to obtain this objective.

Abraham was selected to join the officers' corps. Having
completed his officer's training course, he was put in charge
of instructing recruits and assigned to defend a district on
the outskirts of Tel Aviv bordering several Arab villages. As
he himself said, his strengths were not on the political, ideo-
logical side. "My involvement came more on the practical
side."

The riots in which Abraham and Hodes had almost been
killed in Nablus marked the onset of a three-year Arab rebel-
lion against the British and the Jews. In Abraham's sector of
Tel Aviv, two Jews were killed at the Herzl Street rail crossing,
and Abraham was assigned to the Irgun team that was chosen
to enact the retaliation. "I was not in the unit that was doing the actual firing, but [in] the preparatory actions and the
actions of the security that was attached to that, to get those
people who were involved in the real shooting on the train,
getting them away from that area to safer areas." Two Arabs
were killed in the action, but the police had surrounded the
area, and the getaway car was identified and traced to the
Irgun. Abraham and another conspirator were advised to
take "all the usual, necessary precautions." His commanders
suggested that he leave the country for a while, and made him

two offers—he could go either to Italy or to South Africa to continue his studies. If he went to Italy he would have had to keep a low profile, but South Africa offered him the opportunity to do important fund-raising work for the organization and to prepare for Jabotinsky's imminent visit to that country. Accompanied by his friend Shlomo Rebanenko, whom he had recruited into the Jewish paramilitary, he sailed from Aden to Durban, South Africa, aboard the freighter *Landeck Castle*. Abraham's parents, who had no idea whatsoever of his involvement in the revisionist paramilitary, helped with the boat fare.

In Johannesburg, Abraham was compelled to take a job to support himself and was able to study only part-time. His principal and preferred activity was organizing meetings and raising funds, "mainly for the purchase of arms, if possible." He seems to have offended some of his fellow students with the booklets he produced, which were stamped with the Irgun emblem of a rifle superimposed on a map of Palestine and the motto *Rak Kach*—"Only Thus." Whatever the cause, his campus recruitment activities were not very successful, and he moved out of his student lodgings to work full-time for the organization as a lecturer, activist, and propagandist for the Zionist publication *The Eleventh Hour*. "You can imagine my studies were at an end; I was fully qualified already at what I was doing." He was appointed to act as Jabotinsky's guide and bodyguard when the great man arrived in South Africa. His plan was to return to Palestine as soon as politically and financially feasible.

It was at this time that he met Essie in a Hebrew-speaking

circle, and they were married in 1938. Abraham, by his own admission, was "penniless" in those days, without enough money even to pay for his and Essie's passage to Palestine. In any case, Essie had emigrated from pogrom-torn Lithuania only ten years earlier, traumatized and without a word of English, and had found a stable, welcoming home in Africa; understandably, she was reluctant to begin their new life together by uprooting herself yet again on such a precarious footing. Moreover, Abraham was technically in South Africa illegally and was denied residency. Thus, along with Essie's parents, her sister Kiki, and Kiki's husband, Emo, they moved on to the city of Bulawayo, a major business and industrial hub in the British colony of Southern Rhodesia, with the intention of saving enough money for an eventual return to Palestine. "Essie was very attached to her parents, and I had the feeling at that time that it wouldn't be fair on my part to insist on the move to proceed to Palestine, having been involved in the activities of the Irgun a little bit, and Essie being . . . It would have been wrong on my part to do that. Essie wasn't so involved politically as I was, and I felt that it would bring some hardship upon her unless she would be able to devote her life the way I tended to devote mine at the time."

Abraham found work as a bookkeeper at an auto dealership, across the street from a bicycle shop owned by Philip Lieberman, whose brother-in-law Abraham had met on the *Landeck Castle*. It was 1939, and the situation in Palestine had deteriorated to the extent that Abraham was very anxious to return. But Essie was now pregnant with Hertzie, and with any return home precluded by the outbreak of World War II,

in 1940 he took a job with Lieberman, only to enlist shortly
thereafter in the Rhodesian armed forces. He was trained as a
machine gunner, and in 1941 his unit sailed on the *Mauritania*
for Egypt, where it was absorbed into the Second Cheshire
Battalion and saw action alongside the Second Gurkhas. They
were briefly stationed in Palestine, between Acre and Lebanon, in preparation for an assault on Iran via Syria that never
took place, before returning to Egypt, where Abraham was
inducted into the British Intelligence Corps on the basis of
his knowledge of Russian and Arabic.

At first, he was offered a post in Murmansk, supervising
documents and equipment being shipped to the Soviets, but
being Russian-born he was very reluctant to put himself into
their hands. Instead, he accepted a position in Rayak, in the
Bekaa Valley of Lebanon, where the rail line from Cairo to
Iraq switched from a wide gauge to a narrow gauge and all
goods had to be unloaded and reloaded into new cars. He
spent the winter and summer of 1943 in Lebanon, much awed
by its beauty, before returning once again to Cairo. During
this time, he was often able to see his family and friends in
Palestine on brief visits that were filled with joy and pain.
Many of his friends from the Irgun, including the notorious
district commander Benyamin Zeroni, had been deported by
the British to the Gilgil internment camp in Kenya.

In 1944, having contracted bilharzia in Egypt, Abraham
was shipped back to Rhodesia for treatment. Reunited with
Essie for the first time in almost four years, this was his first
meeting with his daughter, Hertzie, my wife's mother. Following operations to remove his infested appendix and ton-

sils, his war was over. "I came back from Egypt with the rank of sergeant major, and our life now starts again in Rhodesia." Nevertheless, he remained haunted by the time he had spent with his parents and brothers and their families in Palestine, and even now his heart and soul called on him to go home.

Philip Lieberman offered him his old bookkeeping job in Bulawayo, but Abraham was determined to strike out on his own, believing that he would not be able to save the money he needed to return to Palestine if he was anyone's employee. Instead, in a fifty-fifty partnership with Lieberman, he opened his own bicycle dealership in the Rhodesian capital, Salisbury (now Harare), which he ran successfully until the Zimbabwean war of independence compelled them to leave the country in 1977.

And what of his dream of returning to Palestine? Abraham remained highly active and rose to prominence in the Revisionist political opposition of the Zionist movement in Africa. In the brief biography he recorded for us, he glosses over it with acerbic humor. "I continued to act, devoting greater time, but it was really in a way . . . let me say openly, it was laughable. I became like a salon Zionist, the same way in the days when the communist movement in South Africa or other Western European countries they could only sit at home in the salons and talk about their support for communism. They were called the 'salon communists.' So I gradually became a salon Zionist." Once the State of Israel was born in 1948, "Well, now they could do without me. I could only continue to look after my own affairs from an economic point of view, making the possibility for me with my small family in

Rhodesia, giving the opportunity for Essie to be close to her aging, failing parents, and Hertzie to have her own way to start planning her own life." These were not real or plausible explanations for why he failed to follow through on what, until then, had been the single most important impulse of his life, and he didn't even try to give them a convincing gloss. The fact was, plain and simple, that Essie did not want to live in Israel, and so they didn't go. They spent time there every year with Abraham's growing tribe of nieces, nephews, grandnieces, and grandnephews, and they even bought a small apartment in Ra'anana, but Abraham would never live in the Holy Land again.

Having spent six hours telling the story of his life into our microphone, he ended it all with a joke.

Now to complete the story of our life in Rhodesia and South Africa. Well, I don't think we will go to any countries, as from my experience I don't think any other country will let us in. When we were in Russia, it culminated in the revolution. When we arrived in Rhodesia, there again it culminated in a revolution for liberty. In South Africa, the same thing happened since we've been there since 1977. Another two countries that we used to go on holidays to, Mozambique and Northern Rhodesia, now they're liberated. Revolutions took place. So I seem to be carrying a germ of revolutions, so I had better stay where I am now without attempting to travel to other countries.

I'm not sure how common it is to believe that one's life can be divided into two distinct parts. I conducted an informal

straw poll among my friends and acquaintances, but the results were inconclusive. Most of those who identified a definite before and after phenomenon in their own lives cited an
illness, divorce, or childbirth as the watershed event. A larger
number recognized a series of events, either rites of passage
or a sequence of cascading traumas, but rejected the idea that
their adult lives had been marked by one overriding moment
of irreversible change. In any case, there was no clear majority for or against the idea, which suggests that at least a
significant minority of people do entertain the notion, even
if it is sometimes a fictional construct that makes sense of
certain abstract paradigms they entertain about themselves.
Take me, for instance. I long struggled with the idea that my
own life was clearly divisible between the time before I took
a job in the civil service—the first three-fifths—and everything that came afterward. Like an air traffic controller, I
thought I could discern a very clear diversion of the trajectory
of my life on the radar screen of my personal history occurring at that precise moment, as if I had been dislodged from
my natural flight path by a missile or an errant bird, but that
is based on an obviously erroneous and willful misreading of
cause and effect. Taking the job wasn't necessarily a cause at
all; it could just as easily have been the effect of some other
unknown, unknowable, or unwelcome cause. I was married
less than a year before I took the job; I turned thirty only
three months after I took the job; my first daughter was born
only eighteen months after I took the job. So why, amid all
this life-altering change, did I see the job as the watershed
event? Wasn't it much more likely that, all unbeknownst to

myself, I was simply engaged in some sort of other process of metamorphosis (in the zoological sense) in which taking a job was just one more facet of the new differentiation? And yet, twenty-two years after the fact, knowing all this, I continued to insist that it was taking the job that had changed my life forever. I clung to it as if the knowledge would save me, most probably because I continued to embrace the analogous fallacy that quitting my job would change everything again, and maybe even change me back to what I was before.

All you think you know for certain is who you were, and what you lost or had deliberately shed, at the moment everything changed. You are convinced that that last image of the former you is indelibly etched upon your soul, like a VIN number that remains unaltered, and mostly hidden, no matter how often a car changes hands. You know who you were then, and how different you are now from that person. And that holds true whether you perceive the change as having been positive or negative. Most commonly, or at least most stereotypically, a man rues the lost, carefree bachelor he was before he married and had children, but if, instead, he had been sad, lost, and lonely before his marriage saved him, he remembers that person just as sharply. I've said this before, but the clarity of that memory, and the conviction of its truth, are blatantly delusional. You're kidding yourself if you imagine you know who you were or what you were thinking all those years ago. I remember myself as I was then only in the way it is useful to me now to remember; who I really was is irrelevant, as is the fact of whether any real change ever took place. The only thing that matters is that *I* believe that a change took place, because change is growth, and if I grew once, and outgrew one larval stage, I can do it again. It's a little like clinging to a leaky raft adrift at sea and convincing yourself it's a surfboard. It may offer you some comfort, but it won't get you very far. As André Aciman has written, "There is no past; there are just versions of the past."

When I look back on Abraham's life, I want to chop it in two the way I used to divide my own life, into a before phase and an after phase. The before phase would be before he met Essie and devoted all his love and passion to the Zionist cause; the after phase would be when he gave up all hope of returning to his beloved Palestine and spent the rest of his life as a mild-mannered family man growing his bicycle shop into a thriving provincial enterprise. For some reason, seeing his life through that lens satisfies some need in me—a need I can only conclude is neurotic, transferential, and sublimating. In other words, I seem yet again to want to comfort myself for my own perceived failings and weaknesses by associating them with the life of someone I admire. I seem to be seeing Abraham through so many different lenses overlaid one upon the other that it is doubtful that I will ever be able to know if I am seeing him clearly, as if I were trying to give myself an eye exam without any training in how to use an optometrist's phoropter. The point being, I think and hope, that by trying to sort out my feelings about Abraham, I will come to some sort of understanding about myself.

Nevertheless, even if you believe that it is totally bogus and self-serving to divide a life—especially someone else's life— into neat consecutive phases just to satisfy some pathological need for balance, it's hard to deny the really dramatic differences between Abraham's first three decades and his last seven. The first reads like some amazing adventure story, set in a world that was part horror show, part wide-open panorama of unimaginable freedoms—a world in which people hid in haylofts from marauding thugs, undertook perilous four-month treks through hostile territory just to escape their own homeland, eluded murderous rioters by fleeing out the back doors of palaces; but it was also a place where even an undereducated immigrant could find his way in a new world and take part in building a new country and defining its values; where he could simply hop on a ship, penniless and practically undocumented, to forge a new identity in a distant, unknown continent; where he could sign up as a spy for the British Empire merely by expressing the desire to do so. No matter what you may think of Abraham's political priorities and possible misdeeds, it's hard to deny that he led a bold, exciting and comparatively uncompromising existence until he reached his mid-twenties. He knew who he was and what he wanted, and he seemed eminently equipped to obtain it. And then he fell in love.

Here is the argument: Abraham loved Palestine and the Zionist cause with an avowed, consuming passion. He had dedicated himself to this passion from the moment of his political awakening, taken great personal risks to advance it, kept it a secret from his own parents, undertaken acts of desperation and perhaps violence that were surely repugnant to his essentially gentle nature, and ultimately endured a painful exile rather than betray it. And even in exile, he had dreamed and worked for years with only one aim—to return to the place that was his familial, ancestral, and spiritual home. But within just a few years of falling in love, that had all dropped by the wayside. Did he really renounce the dream, as he claimed, because Essie was attached to her parents? "I had the feeling at that time that it wouldn't be fair on my part to insist on the move to proceed to Palestine, having been involved in the activities of the Irgun a little bit, and Essie being . . ." His voice trailed off; he was unable to find the word he was looking for. Essie being what? Reluctant? Afraid? Stubborn? What was it about Essie that persuaded Abraham that it was better to become a salon Zionist, a designation that he himself held in evident disdain, and to abandon his life's work, than to push and promote his own agenda? He says, "I felt that it would bring some hardship upon her unless she would be able to devote her life the way I tended to devote mine at the time." On the face of it, this is all backward. He seems to be saying that because she had no overriding passion of her own, it was unfair to ask her to share in his. In a loving relationship, we would normally expect the lesser objection to give way to the dominant motif. The concert pianist does not give up the stage because her husband dislikes staying in hotels. If she did, we would probably conclude that there was an unhealthy imbalance of power between the couple. And so with Abraham it sounds, at least superficially, as if he is making excuses for his own weakness—that Essie had insisted on having things her way, and that he hadn't had the strength to deny her, and had had to reverse engineer a plausible alibi that he could live with, with manifestly mixed results.

This was a story I, too, had long learned how to live with, much as I had learned to live with the idea that I, too, gave up something irredeemable when I renounced the bohemian life, also for reasons that were no clearer in retrospect than they were at the time. I clung to this story about myself because it gave me plausible deniability for my other failures, or perceived failures. It was much easier for me to believe, when I found myself dissatisfied with the outcome of choices I had freely made, that I had once made a mistake that was the source of any subsequent woes. Not a successful novelist? I should never have taken that job. Not always as patient a father as I might be? I should never have taken that job. Not as attentive or as accommodating a husband as I should like to be? I should never have taken that job. Not able to experience the joy or gratitude that a life like mine should inspire? I should never have taken that job. With me, it was a job in the civil service; you can substitute "taken that job" with your own fork in the road, and it comes to exactly the same thing. I should never have gotten married so young. Rejected that transfer. Moved to that city. Had a third child. Smoked that first cigarette. Turned down his proposal. Accepted that first bribe. Skied that double black diamond. Taken that job.

The before and after scenario can be very seductive. It explains so much while reducing the complexities of adulthood to a simple child's equation. Everything was going so well until this happened. I was on my way to fame and fortune, right on track for personal fulfillment, until I took a wrong turn, and nothing has ever been the same since. My work, my family life, my self-esteem, my capacity for joy and wonder, would have been altogether different, and better, had I made the more enlightened decision, but I didn't, and that is why I find myself unable to grope my way out of this dark woods through which I find myself stumbling in midlife. I note, in passing, that this is not about blaming someone else; it's about taking full responsibility for one's own decisions, and perhaps taking too much responsibility, or responsibility for the wrong decision. In a way, it is about scapegoating yourself precisely for the one thing that you ought to go easy on yourself for.

The truth, when you get right down to it, is that nothing was truly going well for Abraham and for me before we made the decisions that apparently changed our lives forever. In his case, his militant activities had brought him to the point of living a double lie—first, by concealing his paramilitary avocation from his beloved parents, and second by convincing himself that he was not engaged in genuine violence because he was not the triggerman. And then, having been hounded from the land of his birth into a frightening, unsettled new world as a child, he was forced to relive that trauma as an adult. Once again, he found himself cast into exile, and this time it was his own actions that had brought the calamity upon him. Is it any wonder that, given the opportunity to stabilize the ever-shifting ground beneath his feet by choosing domesticity and love far from the raging battle, he had at last chosen to do so? He must have recognized that such an opportunity would not come his way again—that if he undermined or abandoned the one relationship of his life that promised true happiness and true healing, he could not ever again hope for another. It was indeed a before and after decision after all, but with all the burden of resignation and paralysis now on the "before" side, and all the radiance of love and hope on the "after." Not even Ze'ev Jabotinsky could blame him for the choice he made.

Obviously, I did not grow up in the upheaval of the Russian Revolution or the Zionist struggle for a Jewish homeland, but in some ways my situation had much in common with Abraham's at the time when, at roughly the same age, I made the decision to opt for love and tranquility. Like him, without knowing it I was searching for a way to heal a wound and pacify a trauma that had long festered and threatened to poison the entirety of my emotional being. In my case, it was the disintegration of my parents' marriage when I was ten and the simultaneous onset of my mother's malignant multiple sclerosis, which brought on the five-year physical and psychological collapse that led to her death in 1976. My siblings and I, often left to our own devices in dealing with this catastrophe, developed a variety of survival strategies—all predicated on the suppression of guilt, anger, despair, and grief—that have continued to resonate and trip us up deep into our own adulthoods.

Having essentially sleepwalked through my teens and early twenties, I was nowhere near in possession of a conscious understanding of the scope of my emotional debility—or even, frankly, that there was anything wrong with me at all—when I met Judy, but I must have intuited my own need and her unique capacity to fill it. Never having been in therapy, I'm not sure how I figured out that if I could only have a do-over—but this time with all the health, guidance, support, and security that had been lacking the first time—I just might be able to dispel the pall that seemed to overhang my days and even the most heartening of my achievements. I chose to love and be loved, and it's almost impossible at this stage to imagine that I ever wondered whether I made the right choice.

As I mentioned right from the start, my grandfather-in-law Abraham never expressed a moment of doubt or regret for any important decision he ever made, and certainly not for *the* decision. He may have entertained inner qualms that he did not share with the rest of us, but if you had asked him outright why he had never returned to live in Palestine, I think he would have said, purely and simply, that he did what he did for love. He certainly never seemed to berate or second-guess himself, and absolutely never suggested that his life had at any time taken a wrong turn. It had taken a turn, for sure, but it had been the right turn. He was able to make fun of himself as a salon Zionist because it was a far gentler self-appraisal than it would have been if he had chosen politics over love. In this world, we tend to forgive almost anything if it is done for love; suddenly, Abraham's apparent weakness can be seen as his greatest strength.

I write about Abraham because his was an exemplary life, and because I believe it sheds light on the dilemma that so many of us face, especially as we reach this threshold of an age at which we are able to look backward and forward at the same time. I write about myself for the same reason—not because I somehow imagine that the life of a middle-age writer in crisis has anything to teach anyone else about the wisdom of owning and embracing one's choices, especially those that are most problematic, but precisely because in my failure to grasp the obvious lessons that my life has offered me I know I share that incapacity with so many thoughtful, restless minds. On the one hand, I look at Abraham and I associate him with all my own fears and desires so as to reduce his life to an object lesson for my personal consumption; on the other, I attribute all sorts of wisdoms to him that may simply reflect the aspirational delusion that we can all achieve life-long happiness in the most basic of paradigms human existence has to offer. There was the time before, when we were happy; and the time after, when we were not. Contrarily, we were unhappy before, and are happy after. Either way, we see a break in the continuity of our lives that is somehow responsible for our current condition. To return to the image of life as a moving blip on the circular radar screen of some otherworldly air traffic controller, no one would ever want to see a sudden and dramatic deviation from a charted flight path. That would almost certainly indicate a problem, a crisis, an imminent disaster, or a last-minute evasion of disaster. The most desirable radar profile would be a smooth, gently curving arc moving predictably and with purpose toward a final destination.

In his *History of the English Church*, the eighth-century Northumbrian monk Bede writes of King Edwin's deliberations with his counselors about the wisdom and advisability of converting to Christianity. One thane compares our life to the flight of a bird:

Your majesty, when we compare the present life of man on earth with that time of which we have no knowledge, it seems to me like the swift flight of a single sparrow through the banqueting-hall where you are sitting at dinner on a winter's day with your thanes and counselors. In the midst there is a comforting fire to warm the hall. Outside, the storms of winter rain or snow are raging. This sparrow flies swiftly in through one door of the hall, and out through another. While he is inside, he is safe from winter storms; but after a few moments of comfort, he vanishes from sight into the wintry world from which he came. Even so, man appears on earth for a little while; but of what went before this life or of what follows, we know nothing.

The image is meant to evoke the attractions of Christianity for those who fear oblivion, but the metaphor of our brief lives as the arc of a flying sparrow, both beginning and ending in darkness, is one we all recognize and approve, I believe. It encapsulates all the mystery, grace, ease, and painlessness that we hope will define our own lives, as well as the sense of brevity and displacement that shadows our every move. It is a beautiful vision, but if Edwin's unnamed adviser had described the far more likely and familiar scenario of a bird accidentally flying into an enclosed space, being panicked by the noise, light, and heat, frantically but fruitlessly beating its wings against the walls and rafters until it ultimately breaks its neck trying to escape, all its utility as a metaphor for comfort in an enigmatic universe would have been lost. We want to see the span of our lives as the unbroken arc of a bird in flight because it evokes all the sense of wonder, effortlessness, joy, peace, and movement unburdened by physical limitations and moral responsibility that we feel when we watch an actual sparrow or lark sweep across our field of vision. There would be something deeply wrong and troubling if that bird were to suddenly encounter an immovable obstacle in midflight.

But that, of course, is the way most of us live our lives. Encountering obstacles, bumping into them, and picking ourselves up off the floor, or circumventing them, or pretending they don't exist, or blaming them for everything that has gone wrong or could go wrong in the future, or blaming ourselves or someone else for placing them in our path. We are not carefree birds unloosed by gravity, no matter how much we might wish to be. We are earthbound plodders barely able to see beyond our own noses; clumsy, unsubtle, and harmless at best, more often grasping, destructive, and willfully purblind to the needs of those closest to us. And when we see a bird fly by, we may be just as likely to reach up in an attempt to bring it down than to allow it to sweep past unmolested to its unknown destination.

After having misread him for so long, I see now that Abraham was just such a bird. Nobody can accuse him of having lived a brief life, or an unlovely one, but certainly in my myopia I tried to bring him down nonetheless. Essie was not an obstacle in his path, but an open window that he flew through elegantly and gratefully. It has taken me some time to see that. I can only hope that I will one day come to see all my own perceived obstacles as the open windows they most certainly are.

Playing the Lottery

I don't want to accept an idea of life where the success of the self is measured by the success of the written page." These are the words of Elena Ferrante, an Italian novelist who is probably best known in the United States as the author of *The Days of Abandonment*. To be precise, they are the words of an author who goes by the name of Elena Ferrante. Nobody knows who she is, or even for sure if the author is really a woman, despite massive speculation, especially in Italy, where her work is very popular and two films have already been made of her books. According to James Woods, who wrote about her for *The New Yorker*, "she grew up in Naples, and has lived for periods outside Italy. She has a classics degree; she has referred to being a mother." And that is the sum total of all that is known about her—an achievement that, in this day and age of total awareness and total entitlement, betrays nothing short of a herculean act of will and dissimulation. The lady really does not want to be found.

When Robert Galbraith, the author of *The Cuckoo's Calling*, was revealed to be the pseudonym of J. K. Rowling, the creator of the Harry Potter series, some people (not including me) believed the entire setup to be a publicity stunt. The conspiracy theory was that the "cover-up" and revelation—supposedly against the author's wishes but secretly prearranged—would bring even more attention to the book than if it had been released under the author's name. That didn't make much sense to me, especially given the potential for such a shoddy ploy to backfire on its author. Rowling does not need to resort to subterfuge to publicize her books. It is far more likely that she, who can do pretty much anything she wants without asking her publisher's permission, wanted to know (or prove to herself) whether she could write and publish an adult book on its own merits, free of any bias in favor of or against the world's most successful author. In the end, of course, she got the best of both worlds.

But Elena Ferrante has adhered to her no-publicity stance since before the publication of her first book, *Troubling Love*, in the early 1990s. It's no publicity stunt; she's in it for the long haul, and she withdrew from public scrutiny long before she had anything to gain by refusing to promote her own work. The abridged version of her philosophy reflects a kind of austere, idealistic, *Field of Dreams* conviction that books "have no need of their authors." If you write it, they will read. She decided that her work would have to sink or swim without her. "If [books] have something to say, they will sooner or later find readers; if not, they won't." Such obstinacy would have an American publisher tearing his hair out, but it has worked well for Ferrante and seems to have proven correct her dictum that a *good* book will find its audience. Ferrante's books do just fine "without" her; if someone else's doesn't, well . . .

need she say more? If you fail, it's your own fault for writing a bad book; don't blame your publicist.

But Ferrante's rejection of common marketing wisdom goes further. She believes that if she were to allow herself to be engaged in selling her work, she would in effect be selling herself. "The editorial marketplace is in particular preoccupied with finding out if the author can be used as an engaging character and thus assist the journey of his work through the marketplace. If one yields, one accepts, at least in theory, that the entire person, with all his experiences and his affections, is placed for sale along with the book." In this reading, she almost seems to be accusing her editor of being the enemy, the capitalist exploiter, if not actually trying to pimp her. A better understanding of that dynamic, I feel, would help her see that the author can, in certain circumstances, be the most eloquent and trustworthy champion of her own work, and that her role in marketing is better compared to that of reverend spokesperson than to car-show model, or whore. The relationship between author and sales force will be sordid only if the author allows or encourages it to be so.

If Ferrante were Rowling, or some nonfiction juggernaut, it would be almost impossible for her to maintain her anonymity for as long as she has. The only thing that has protected her through twenty years of publishing is that, curious as they may be, there are not many people out there who are prepared to devote the resources and expertise necessary to outing a publicity-shy literary novelist. Who would gain by it? Even so, it must take a fair amount of energy and devotion for the author behind the Ferrante name to keep her identity secret in the era of the Anonymous collective. Can it be worth all the time and effort? I ask this question knowing that Ferrante has documented her quest for anonymity in a brief publication called *Fragments*, which her publishing house distributes for free in a variety of electronic formats, including for Amazon's Kindle reader. I don't deny for one minute that *Fragments*, like most all of Ferrante's writing, makes for very compelling reading, but it serves essentially as a clever, literary publicity brochure for Ferrante's books. Ferrante and her publishers have, in effect, managed to turn her insistence on anonymity and her refusal to participate in the marketing of her books into a very effective and original marketing strategy.

Many writers, when confronting the unexpected failure of a project to which they have devoted several years of their lives, look outward for the cause, firing their agents or blaming their publicist or publisher. That is not my way, and would not be even if I did not adore my agent and my publicist. The first question I ask myself is what I did wrong; the second thing I say to myself is that the book is not as good as it should have or could have been, because I wrote it at four in the morning. Unfortunately, given the limited hours available to me to write on the weekdays, if I had devoted the time and attention the book needed to become what it ought to have been, it would have taken twelve years to write instead of four. By that calendar, after twenty years of writing I would now be only in the middle of the first draft of my second book, but at least I would have assured myself that I had done everything possible to nurture my work to its fullest potential. Most people, including me, would probably see this as the preferable scenario—write one great book instead of four decent ones. But how can you know? On the one hand, Donna Tartt publishes one book roughly every decade, and that works extremely well for her. James Joyce, too, was a paragon of patience and humble self-confidence who lived in relative poverty and obscurity for decades and who, although very ambitious for his work, never let his ambition get in the way of what he needed to do. On the other hand, Henry Roth published his masterpiece *Call it Sleep* in 1934 with every intention of pursuing a traditional career as a novelist, but the book's mixed reception disheartened him so thoroughly that he did not produce another for sixty years. By the time *Call it Sleep* was rediscovered and reprinted in 1964, Roth—who had left New York for rural Maine, where, among other things, he raised chickens—had almost entirely lost the habit of thinking of himself as writer. Every career has its own arc, and there would be little profit in trying on a variety of contrasting scenarios in an effort to see which fits best. There are no rules.

In her memoir *This Is the Story of a Happy Marriage*, Ann Patchett describes her eight-year "apprenticeship" as a freelance writer for *Seventeen* magazine before she was able to earn a living as a "real" writer. She didn't make much money at it, but she argues plausibly that the flexibility, discipline, and ability to self-edit that she acquired writing throwaway articles for teenagers have been of great use to her as a literary novelist. Many if not most writers have a similar kink in their story—an often adorable, incongruous account of their uncertain first steps into a world that offers few guidelines and no safety nets, the unworthy day labor that made them who they are, the hard-to-imagine drudgery of the soon-to-be-famous. Virtually every artist's biography, and often the life stories of analogous mavericks in other realms, such as Steve Jobs and Bill Gates, relate some version of this meet-cute first encounter between a genius and her destiny.

Very few of us can realistically compare ourselves to Steve Jobs, or even—no disrespect intended—to Ann Patchett. For every inspiring my-life-as-a-young-dog story, there are ten thousand life histories that are identical in almost every respect right up until the moment the hero or heroine is plucked from obscurity and meets his or her destiny. That is where the stories diverge—the genius gradually or precipitously rises to assume her appointed place among the constellations; the ten thousand remain in the bear pit, lifting their gaze to the hills from whence they expect their help to come, and only slowly—often painfully, pitifully slowly—growing into the realization that it isn't coming. That is essentially what has happened with me and my career. I entered it with every expectation of a glory that has not been forthcoming. Yes, I've more or less written and published the books I've wanted to write, but in the general scheme of things I've had to do a lot of recalibrating of expectations and rewards in order to accommodate myself to my less-than-flattering image in reality's mirror. That's normal, and would be exactly the same no matter what vocation I had pursued, even if writers, and artists in general, tend to see their work as harder than anybody else's.

Virtually all of us are disappointed in some element of our youthful aspirations and delusions about who we are and what we are capable of. Everybody has to learn in his own way and by his own mistakes who he is going to be in the aftermath of this revelation. Many accept it with a shrug and nary a look back; others grow angry, bitter, or resentful, blame anyone but themselves, and project their sense of failure onto the world at large—in other words, they wholly fail to accept their situation, like the hungry ghosts of Chinese folklore; still others continue to hope against hope and spend the interior episodes of their existence in parallel lives of their own edification. But unless we have suffered especially bad luck, most of us will have to learn to live with the fact that our circumstances and accomplishments are largely the results of the choices we have freely undertaken to make.

In *The Courage to Create*, the psychologist Rollo May defines human freedom as "our capacity to pause between the stimulus and response and, in that pause, to choose the one response toward which we wish to throw our weight. The capacity to create ourselves, based upon this freedom, is inseparable from consciousness or self-awareness." By these lights, you are free when you are at liberty to consider dispassionately and without coercion all the options available to you and to select that which best suits you. The person you believe yourself to be is the one you yourself have constructed in the wielding of this freedom. Thus, having, in principle, freely chosen to take a job and, again in principle, freely chosen to remain there all these years, you have constructed your identity in the awareness that you have willingly curtailed what you perceive as your own freedom. You can curse your perceived lack of freedom, you can perpetuate your perceived lack of freedom, you can blame yourself alone for your perceived lack of freedom, and yet you can still consider yourself to be an agent of free will. This is a paradox that underlies so much of our daily existence, and our perception of ourselves and our place in the world, without our even being aware of its agency.

Like most people outside the world of Internet activism, I had never heard of Aaron Swartz until he took his own life in 2013 at the age of twenty-six. At the time of his death, Swartz was facing federal wire fraud charges, which carried a potential sentence of thirty-five years in jail, for illegally downloading academic journal articles from the JSTOR digital library. By all accounts a programming prodigy, Swartz was a coinventor of the RSS web feed format at the age of fourteen and an early owner of Reddit, the sale of which to Condé Nast made him a wealthy man for a while. All his life, but especially in his final years, he was intensely dedicated to the kind of freedom-of-information causes that led to his liberation of the JSTOR articles and many other government documents, legally and otherwise. He was a man who spent a lot of time thinking about freedom and its ramifications.

I have no interest at all in making capital of the senseless and unnecessary tragedy of Swartz's suicide, which has nothing to do with the issues being explored here. I wish only to quote one brief statement he made, as reported by Larissa

MacFarquhar in *The New Yorker* not long after his death. As recounted by a close friend, in response to her suggestion that he could easily find a high-earning job to pay off the debts incurred in the course of his legal troubles, Swartz said: "I would rather sleep on friends' couches for the rest of my life than take a job I don't want." At the same time, several of those closest to him suggested that, as his money evaporated, one of his greatest fears was becoming dependent on his friends, and that this dread may have been a factor in his decision to end his life. So, if nothing else, it's clear in this instance that someone whose life is dedicated to the pursuit, protection, and expansion of freedom can be confused and intellectually conflicted about what it actually means—and what it truly demands of those who embrace it. For all his precocious experience, thoughtfulness, and generosity of spirit, not to mention his dynamic approach to liberating knowledge for use by all, it's remarkably sad and mystifying to see how limited and fear-driven he was in championing his own personal freedom. He so intimately associated the idea of taking a job he didn't want, even on a limited basis, with a loss of freedom that, in fleeing it, he ended up throwing himself into the maw of a far more restrictive prison. We all want to be free, I guess, even when we haven't the faintest idea of what we mean by "freedom" or what living a free life would even look like.

|||||||||||||||||||||||||||||||||||||||||||

My wife steadfastly refuses to play the lottery game. In a display of puritanism and humorlessness that can be a little shocking in someone who otherwise engages very happily with her own active imagination, she actually seems to be offended by the very idea of the game. Why, she asks, should she have any interest in pretending that she has just won a vast fortune, and that she can now have anything and everything she ever wanted, when she already has everything she needs and is by all reasonable standards perfectly content and provided for? I tell her that it's just a game—playing it doesn't indicate some deep, existential void in your soul, or some streak of insatiable greed. It's just for fun. Even the Dalai Lama and Saint Francis of Assisi could play it, because it allows you to give all your (imaginary) millions away to the neediest people or communities in the world, or to serve the noblest causes in a way that you almost certainly will never get the chance to do in real life. She usually ends up recognizing that her inflexibility in the matter is a little silly, or at least disproportionate, but she still won't play. So I play it alone, in my head, when I'm walking the dog or biking to work. And as many will attest, it's one of the few games for adults that's just as much fun to play alone as it is in company.

It's hard to believe that my fantasy is much different from anyone else's. First I dispense with the usual logistical issues, like is it safe to call my accountant with the news, or do I have to go down to his office and tell him in person? How do I keep my ticket safe until I cash it in? What is the minimum I will need not just to win but also to keep, after taxes, in order to make the game worth playing? If I win two million dollars, for instance, I get to keep one million after taxes, so once I've paid off my debts and shared my good fortune with my loved ones there's barely enough left over for a relaxed dinner for four at Le Bernardin. Remember, this is a fantasy game about freedom, not greed. My imaginary winnings need to be expansive enough to give my imagination some room to breathe, but they can't be so unlimited that I can have anything I want, because prioritizing is what gives the game its tension. It takes forethought and sensitivity to get these things right; but once these issues are out of the way, I get down to the nitty-gritty.

The first order of business is to determine who gets a slice of my newfound wealth. Always on my list are my siblings and siblings-in-law, my father and my parents-in-law. Things get a little fuzzy after that. For instance, do I include my nieces and nephews, who, after all, are already getting a share through their parents? What about Judy's cousins and their children, with whom we are almost as close as brothers and sisters? What about dear friends, especially the needier ones? Will a gift ruin our friendship or strengthen it? Usually at this point I give up on this aspect of the game because it's not much fun and it starts bogging everything down. After all, freedom should be a gift, not a burden.

After the family come the charities. I have several public institutions and NGOs that I already support, very modestly, and they will get a big chunk. After that, I suppose I will have to sit down and think about starting a foundation so the money can keep giving, but I don't want to spread it too thin. One or two causes at most, so my wealth can have a real impact, but there are just too many good causes that, when I think that I could give to any and all of them, it gives me a headache just thinking about it, so again I put that part off until I will actually need to implement it in real life.

Now whatever is left of my winnings is mine to spend on myself as I please. And this is where the game starts to get boring. Playing the lottery game is like ordering Chinese food—you always forget, until it's too late, why you swore you'd never do it again the last time you did it. I can never think of anything new I want, except for maybe slightly bigger and better versions of the things I already have.

The only thing I really want is to be free to write without having to worry about how to pay the rent, but that part— the quitting-my-job part—never varies from one game to the next. Just because a person likes to play a certain game doesn't necessarily mean he's good at it. Other people might go wild, which is the whole point of the game I suppose, but I genuinely can't ever imagine owning a yacht, or my own plane, or a Lamborghini, or a suite at the Mayfair, or whatever it is that takes the kind of money that is available only to Russian oligarchs and lottery winners. Most of the things I would want to buy I could buy now if I paid off my debts and earned a little bit more than I do. It's not that I'm not greedy and selfish; I am both, but not really for things that can be bought with money, unless you count free time and solitude, which although they cannot be assigned a monetary value on the free market, are very much for sale.

So why do I even bother playing this stupid, venal game? I think again of the psychologist Adam Phillips. "In our un-lived lives," he writes, "we are always more satisfied, far less frustrated versions of ourselves." That seems very right to me—that when we fantasize these parallel or alternate lives, it's not about satisfying frustrated desire but about creating a universe that will allow us to be our best selves. I fantasize about winning the lottery—I allow myself to fantasize about winning the lottery—not because I want all the things the money could buy me, but because a universe in which I win the lottery is a universe where I am not pulled in a dozen different directions at the same time, where I can focus solely on what interests me, where there is enough room to breathe, so that I don't always need to feel that the time and attention I devote to my own needs are stolen from someone else. I am the better person that I always imagined I could be if I did not have to dole out stingy little parcels of myself until there is nothing left. I am happier, kinder, less fearful, more generous, more patient, and less resentful because I can finally afford to be. I am my best self. I've just won the lottery.

When the American poet Jack Gilbert died in 2012, I knew almost nothing about him but was drawn to his biography by the emphasis all his obituaries placed on the independent, solitary way he had lived his life. Gilbert intrigued me because he seemed to embody something I had been groping to define, and I began to read more about him in the wake of his death. He'd bypassed all the conventional markers of the literary life—schooling, degrees, literary conferences and colonies, networking, logrolling, constant publishing, teaching, and so on—and spent much of his life overseas in self-conscious isolation from his peers, as a traveling lecturer, doing odd jobs, or just living off the kindness and hospitality of friends. The word "fierce"—as in "a poet who has remained fierce in his avoidance of the beaten path"—often comes up in descriptions of Gilbert. In the words of one breathless admirer, Gilbert was "the poet who stands outside his own time, practicing a poetics of purity in an ever-more cacophonous world." One NPR interviewer summed up the general feeling about what made Gilbert different from all the other poets: "In the end, he was not interested in being a famous poet; he just wanted to be true to himself." As someone who has spent an entire lifetime trying to be true to himself, I can attest to the fact that it's not as easy as it sounds. In my experience, most of us struggle just trying to figure out what it even means to be true to ourselves. But Gilbert knew just what being true to himself would entail: "Gilbert's literary celebrity seemed assured—until he turned his back on it." His chief concern seemed to be that seeking or even acknowledging worldly success would be little more than a distraction from the life he was born to lead and the work he was born to produce, so he removed himself from temptation. And yet, despite his indifference to the world, the world could not remain indifferent to him—Gilbert was showered with fellowships, awards, two Pulitzer nominations, effusive praise, and photo spreads in *Glamor* and *Vogue*. None of this proved capable of diverting him from his chosen course.

The more I read about Gilbert in my quest to understand something about myself, the more certain I became that he represented everything I imagined a free, bold, fearless artist/man should be. The envy and sense of inadequacy that reading his life story evoked in me convinced me that I was on the right track—this was a man whose example I, and any other freedom-seeker, would be wise to emulate. Above all, he appeared to have been everything I was not: brave, iconoclastic, indifferent to what anyone else thought of him; a passionate soul reverberating to the frequencies of the universe; a bold trailblazer and sneerer at convention; artist as frontiersman, human being as rocket ship, a growling blacksmith at the forge of his own destiny. No hovering parent, paper-pusher, foodie, vacation-taker, subway-rider, middleway-compromiser like me. He seemed to be the real thing at every level. I felt that when in my own life I had pictured the platonic ideal of the artist, or any worker, who was prepared to sacrifice everything and forsake all distractions for the sake of his creative freedom, Gilbert was who I had pictured, even before I had heard of him. Someone who knew how to be true to himself. I suspected that I had something important to learn from him. I wanted Jack Gilbert, in his poems and in his interviews—of which there were quite a few online, surprisingly abundant for a man who had turned his back on the world—to teach me how to "live out a spiritual quest for authenticity."

What would it even mean to be "authentic"? Popular culture is not especially helpful when it comes to defining authenticity. Ronald Reagan, John Wayne, Katharine Hepburn, the Dalai Lama, Julia Child—we call them authentic or genuine because there would seem to be no daylight between their public and private personas; unlike the vast majority of celebrated folk in every walk of life who wear masks in public, the authentic ones are those we deem to be pretty much exactly the way they appear to be. That's all very well if you're a celebrity, but how do the rest of us know if we're authentic? When I imagined trying to measure up against Jack Gilbert there was almost nothing about the way I lived that encouraged me to believe that I had any capacity to identify authenticity in my own life, let alone in the lives of others. I supposed, superficially, that you would first have to be able to know what it was that you genuinely wanted—as opposed to things you were drawn to for subliminal, unhealthy reasons—and then devote yourself exclusively to its pursuit. No creature comforts, no concern for the impression you make on others when you walk in the door or when you walk out, no weak-willed concession to loneliness or desire for recognition, can be allowed to distract you from your quest for this authenticity. And make no mistake, it cannot be discovered in a search, or an inquiry, or a study; it has to be a *quest*—a single-minded, high-minded, transcendent *quest*. Authenticity is big game—the biggest game of all—and can be brought to ground only with the heaviest weaponry. Authenticity is not available to those, like me, who would seek it in their spare time, or while engaged in parallel pursuit of livelihood, security, pleasure, or healing. That is why I didn't even need to ask myself if I could lay any claim to authenticity. It is not an accessory that you can wear with your daily outfits; it is the only piece of clothing you own, because you had first to throw out your entire wardrobe to acquire it, like John the Baptist in his camelhair shift. You cannot be authentic on the weekend and be its opposite, whatever that might be, for the rest of the week, nor can you point to one aspect of your life as proof of authenticity—I am an authentic parent, artist, Buddhist, dog-lover, anarchist—while compromising yourself in all the others. You are either authentic in your entirety or not at all.

The emphasis in the phrase "be true to yourself" has to be on "self." This is not a task for the faint of heart or the easily distracted. First, you have to convince yourself that there really is such a thing as your "self"—a unique, unitary, primordial core of awareness that would be the real you no matter where or when you were born, no matter what family and cultural influences you had been subject to, no matter how much neurotic padding you had wrapped it in. People born in the West, I think, take it for granted that it's in there somewhere, because how could any of us be the singular individuals we are without it? Religious people call it our "soul," the only thing we bring with us when we are born and take with us when we die, but even atheists believe in the self. It is not exactly what we may choose to call our "personality," our "temperament," or our "identity," all of which are contingent and mutable; it is something simultaneously more than the sum of all these and other, hidden facets, and something far less, far more compact—not the molecule, not the atom, not the electron cloud or the nucleus, not the subatomic particles of our consciousness, but the strong force that holds them all together. Psychoanalysts may seek to give names to its various components, but ultimately such atomization has to give way to a quasi-mystical belief in something integral, latent, unseen, and untouchable at our core.

Yet even if we are not entirely sure of what it is, or that we would recognize it if we found it, we nevertheless make it our life's mission to locate it, like conquistadors plunging into the virgin jungle in search of El Dorado. Virtually every milestone of Western civilization, from the *Iliad* to the *Inferno* to *Don Quixote* to *Great Expectations* to *On the Road*, is a variant of this story and a commentary on its evolution over the millennia. In his poetry, Gilbert explicitly identified himself with yet another version—Orpheus perilously descending into the underworld. I knew that I did not have it in me to emulate Orpheus, and that Jack Gilbert did. But could I learn it from Jack?

There is not yet a book-length biography of Gilbert, but if you're interested in his life, a good place to start is the lengthy interview published by the *Paris Review* in 2005, available online, as all *Paris Review* interviews are. The opening paragraph is promising: "It is not unusual for men and women in the audience to tell him how his poems have saved their lives . . . the mystique of a life lived utterly without regard for the conventions of literary fortune and fame." Sarah Fay, the interviewer, reminds Gilbert of the instant success and notoriety that came with the publication of his first collection, *Views of Jeopardy*, in 1962, when the *New York Times* called him "inescapably gifted" and when he was "widely feted by the literary establishment." His response is winning and self-deprecating.

It was shockingly generous. It pleased me. Gordon Lish kindly pushed me. I was proud and grateful, but it didn't change my work much. I enjoyed those six months of being famous. Fame is a lot of fun, but it's not interesting. I loved being noticed and praised, even the banquets. But they didn't have anything that I wanted.

He then goes on to try to explain what it was that he sought to reject, all the while appearing to take pains to avoid judging or condemning his peers.

> *The people who are famous have earned it; they've earned it to an ex-traordinary degree. They've given their lives to it, they're professionals, they work hard, and they raise families. And they're very smart, they stay at their desks all the time—they send out everything. They teach, which is not easy. What they do is important, but there's no way that I would use my life for that.*

This statement is a bit off, it seems to me; it reads as if it were designed for those who like their praise faint, with a strong dash of condescension. Who are these people who stay at their desks all the time? Who is it that sends out everything? How can what they do be important yet at the same time so entirely beneath Gilbert's consideration? And how can he possibly know how all these people live their lives when he has spent the past thirty years living in a shack on the beach, ignoring the literary world and its conceits? Still, if you read on, you may be won over, as I was, by the raw truth contained in what I took to be Gilbert's mission statement:

> *It's almost unfair to have been as happy as I've been. I didn't earn it; I had a lot of luck. But I was also very, very stubborn. I was determined to get what I wanted as a life . . . I'm vain enough to think that I've made a successful life. I've had everything I've ever wanted. You can't beat that.*

It's hard to argue against the idea that the very definition of success is to get everything you want in life, and by his own confession Gilbert seems to have achieved it. What Gilbert claimed to have been seeking was to know that he was awake—alert to his own heartbeat—at all times, and to avoid anything—jobs, social entanglements, deadlines, family obligations—that would distance him from his own immediate experience. Even his poetry took a backseat to the quest for authenticity—he published only four collections in his fifty-year career. Certainly, too, he would have rejected the characterization of his writing as a "career" in any traditional sense. And yet, as you read through the *Paris Review* interview, you begin to grow a little uneasy by the way Gilbert defined himself in relation to the world.

For one thing, his status as a maverick, an outsider, is one that he comes back to again and again and again, almost as if he were trying to convince himself of something. It's not an act; we know that materially and intellectually he really did live his life that way. It's not as if he had first been rejected by the establishment and later made a virtue of necessity, as so many of us do, by ascribing his lack of readers to his own bold refusal to conform to societal norms. Rather, he made an admirable, deliberate choice to pass up the fame and glory that he might so easily have claimed. Everybody knew that about him; it was part of his mystique that his exile was genuine and self-imposed. Why, then, was it so important for him to focus on it so resolutely? We all know people who continually boast about how "crazy" or otherwise idiosyncratic they are, when they are in fact anything but. Their need to see themselves as distinct from the herd seems to arise from a suspicion that they are, in fact, completely undistinguished and indistinguishable—which may or may not be true, but in any case this insecurity would make it difficult for them to see themselves objectively or to credit the evidence of their own senses. Gilbert seems to have been a little like that—always needing to insist on all the ways he was different from everyone else:

> "I didn't visit places; I lived places.
> It makes all the difference in the world."

> "If you don't know, I can't tell you."

> "I don't like the idea of anything creative being mechanical.
> That'll kill you."

> "I failed freshman English eight times."

Seriously? Is it even possible to fail English eight times? And why does Gilbert consider it such a selling point? Why does he believe that it says something important about him? We all know the story that Einstein was a bad math student; it is a myth, but it's a myth that burnishes his reputation as an autodidact whose insights into the universe were not contingent on traditional modes of learning and academic recognition. No one disputes that Einstein was a genius, but the world is filled with geniuses; this story elevates him to the rarefied status of genius sui generis. What distinguished him from the multitude of geniuses was his ability to see things that no one had ever seen before, and to see them in a way that is impeded rather than impelled by mainstream thinking. Gilbert claims a similar mantle: "My mind was not available for the impress of teachers or other people's styles." It's not so much that I would dispute his claim to have been a difficult, willful pupil; or that, so he says, he got into the University of Pittsburgh on the basis of a clerical error; or that he applied for (and won) the Yale Younger Poets Prize by accident. It's just that, in retelling and retailing these stories about himself, Gilbert might give the impression of trying to emphasize his humility, but he is in fact promoting everything that makes him unique and authentic. In so doing, he comes across less as Einstein—who consistently denied the bad-student rumor—and more like the meek, bow-tied everyman who tells everybody how crazy he is. Such a revealed sense of insecurity is in itself a pretty minor and harmless human foible, but it's odd to find it in someone whose public persona is based on his loudly proclaimed indifference to what anyone else thinks about him.

It's not far-fetched to conclude that Gilbert made a fetish of himself early on in his career and that he clung to it at all costs. Instead of an artist who had a clear, confident, articulate vision of his place in the universe, he is someone who built an entire edifice of self-regard by rejecting the so-called literary world and the intellectual approach to literature and poetry, but who never had a distinctive vision to oppose it. Instead, as he slogged through the jungle looking for his self without knowing what he was looking for, Gilbert the Conquistador was dazzled by the discovery of a shining golden artifact, his own ego, and mistook it for his grail. He was like those political extremists who believe that being angry is an acceptable substitute for being right. He was so proud of himself for not being part of the literary tradition or succumbing to the temptations and rewards of conformity that he came to see this pride as the source of his prowess both as a man and as a poet. Why else make constant, tireless references to his own modesty, his own carelessness of money and comfort, his reluctance to discuss himself, as if these were the attributes that had made him a poet? "How can you spend your life on games or intricately accomplished things?" he asks, in which the word "games" stands for everything that isn't as authentic as Jack Gilbert's way of life.

So when the interviewer finally stops asking him about himself and his life, and focuses on the subject of poetry—which is ostensibly why he is being interviewed by the country's premier literary periodical—he almost has to twist himself in knots like a politician trying to avoid answering the question he has been posed.

Q: "What is poetry?"
A: "It's a challenge. It's boring—sometimes. It's maddening. It's impossible. It's a blessing. The craftsmanship, the difficulty of making a poem—rightly, adequately, newly. If nothing else, it's wonderful to be that close to magic."

Gilbert was eighty years old at the time of this interview. It's hard to believe that, given the opportunity to discuss his life's work and to pass on some of the wisdom he has collected in the course of a long, rich, and happy life, this is the best he has to offer. That poetry is a blessing? It's boring—*sometimes*?

But let us for the moment give him the benefit of the doubt. Let's say that Gilbert may not have had anything of great importance to say to an interviewer because he was unused to speaking in public about himself and felt uncomfortable and self-conscious. That he was nervous and eager to please at the same time, like anyone who is not in the habit of airing his personal laundry. That everything important he had to say had already been said in his poetry. That he was a modest man not inclined or given to making pronouncements and passing judgment.

Unfortunately, the rest of the interview does not support that argument. Instead, again and again we find Gilbert dismissing his fellow poets and the vast majority of humankind as sheep, blind followers, and sleepwalkers. He is always careful to dull the blade of his contempt with buffers of nonjudgmental humility, but he's not very good at it. His scorn is too bright a beam to baffle. "I don't think anybody should be criticized because their taste is different from mine. Such poems are extraordinarily deft. There's a lot of art in them. But I don't understand where the meat is." He can't resist the temptation to set up straw men to knock down. "I like ornament at the right time, but I don't want a poem to be made out of decoration. If you like that kind of poetry, more power to you, but it doesn't interest me"—as if there were serious poetry readers out there who like mere ornament and are ready to put up a spirited argument in its defense. He's always imagining sycophants to contrast himself with, as if he needs to continuously bolster his own sense of self by sneering at the comatose masses. But then he disarms your suspicion by praising the people he's disparaging.

> A: *Those people [in the literary community] are in business. They're hardworking.*
> Q: *Don't you work hard?*
> A: *Not in the same meaning as the word hard. I put in a lot of effort because it matters to me. Many of these people who teach would do anything not to teach. I don't have any obligations. I don't have a mortgage. These people are working hard at a great price.*

It's that last sentence—"These people are working hard at a great price"—that sums it up for me, but also explains why I was so upset by this interview; why I took it so personally. First, there's that construction "these people," repeatedly hammered at like coffin nails. Ostensibly, he's talking about his fellow poets and writers, but it is no stretch to interpret "these people" as a sneering reference to anyone who does one thing—i.e., work for a living—when he would rather be doing something else. It is brutally, ignorantly dismissive of a vast, undifferentiated swath of humankind that he has made it his life's mission to discount without trying to understand. I am one of those people "working hard," so I feel slighted and judged, but so were Louise Bourgeois, Johannes Brahms, Vladimir Nabokov, and Titian. What is the "great price" Jack Gilbert believes that we have all paid?

I could never have lived my life the way I have if I had children. There used to be a saying that every baby is a failed novel. I couldn't have roamed or taken so many chances or lived a life of deprivation. I couldn't have wasted great chunks of my life. But that would be a mistake for other people. Fine people. Smart people.

With his "Fine people. Smart people," Gilbert is again trying to have it both ways, but at this point it would be a little naive to accept that he really believes that any of us who lives a standard life building a home, raising children, and working hard is a fine or a smart person, especially when the alternative is to roam and take chances. Here, Gilbert is not just setting up straw poets and artists to knock down; he's moved on from those benighted automatons who love ornament in their poetry and believe that creativity should be mechanical. Instead, he has decided to take on all of us, anyone who has ever decided that there's something to be gained by plugging ourselves into our community (be it that of other artists, our neighbors, or simply our fellow citizens) and making connections with people we may not always understand or appreciate. We know the price we pay to do these things, and sometimes it is great, but Jack Gilbert doesn't know what the fuck he's talking about. For all his claims of being independent and above the fray, he is simply an ignorant snob, sneering at things he doesn't understand because he's afraid they might hold some value that he can't grasp or hope to acquire.

*People miss so much because they want money and comfort and pride,
a house and a job to pay for the house. And they have to get a car. You
can't see anything from a car. It's moving too fast. People take vacations. That's their reward—the vacation. Why not the life? Vacations
are second-rate. People deprive themselves of so much of their lives—
until it's too late.*

Why is it so important to Gilbert to judge and dismiss his
inferiors? Does everyone who buys a car do so out of blind
acquisitiveness, or because they hope to learn something profound about life by looking out the window? What is it that so
upsets him about ordinary people living out their ordinary
lives? And most important, why does he keep talking about
them in his interview, instead of about himself? Does he suspect there's something he has missed in his eighty years? How
can a poet, who at the very least has to know that the true life
of the heart is interior, judge people on the basis of such superficial criteria, and decide that they are wasting their lives?
It may well be that taking vacations is not as rewarding as living your entire life as a vacation, but if you have children,
you need to work, and taking vacations becomes a necessity.
Is it always fun? Do you spend every moment of your waking
life focused on the joy of living and the life source of creative
thought? Probably not. Presumably, that is the "great price"
that Gilbert is so unwilling to pay.

But what Gilbert failed to grasp—and I strongly suspect that
his reason for being so contemptuous of the rest of us is that
he was outraged that the sheep had a broader, deeper, slower,

and more integrated vision than his—is that most of us, even the most obtuse, pay a great price in return for a great reward. If you don't have children, for instance, it's possible that you have cut yourself off from an entire universe of human experience and feeling that may be essential to understanding the human condition. And even if that isn't necessarily true, you must at the very least acknowledge that you're in no position to pass judgment on something you know nothing about. You don't need to be a footloose poet to grasp the potential benefits of parenthood, both as an artist and as a human being alive to the restorative powers of love, but you can be a mechanic or a banker or a fast-food worker and profit from its full value. And that argument is hardly limited to parenthood; you can extend it to any relationship, with a person or a community, in which you have agreed to accept a degree of responsibility that potentially impinges on your individual options—on your freedom, as Gilbert might read it. On the other hand, if you don't understand these things and refuse to inquire into them, you may very well have stunted your potential as a poet. And what good is it to you, and what use are you to the world, to be a free-spirited artist who doesn't understand the first thing about what it means to be a human being? Being a poet like Jack Gilbert is like being a surgeon who has never studied anatomy.

I don't think, even in my unfledged youth, that I would ever have wanted to live like Jack Gilbert lived, or to see the world the way he saw it. But it is a vision, when you don't grasp all its implications or see the emotional handicaps that make it so attractive, that appeals to everyone at varying levels. We all want to have more quiet time to ourselves; even if we happen to love our jobs, we all have days when it would be nicer to go to the beach or take a book and a bottle of wine into the forest; we all have days when we wish our kids would grow up faster and leave us alone for once. And we all know that there are moments when it almost seems possible to throw a few things into our overnight bag, empty the bank account, find ourselves a shack on a Greek island somewhere—and to live out the rest of our lives just like Jack Gilbert. Most of us don't and won't do any of those things, not even once, and there at least Gilbert was right—we do pay a price of some sort.

But I find it almost impossible to believe that Gilbert did not pay a far greater price for the way he chose to live his life. Because if you fail to treat your life as a gift to be shared, you lose all the joy and communion that goes along with the sharing. And I think that is why Gilbert was always going on so much about the superiority of not compromising his lifestyle—because he knew that it may actually be a cop-out rather than a bold trek into the unknown. When you share your life, just as when you share anything of value, you get to consume less of it yourself, but you also get to consume parts of the lives of other people, and that's what it means to be human above all. When your only wish is to consume every last drop of your own life yourself, you don't get even a taste of anyone else's, so how can you hope to understand how people think or what they want? I'm not entirely sure what Gilbert meant when he talked about "taking chances," but it takes a lot more courage to share yourself with others than it does to wall yourself off from every possibility of getting hurt. You almost get the impression that Gilbert had no idea how anybody other than himself thought or felt. Maybe that's all he wanted—to understand himself, and nothing more; not to reach out beyond that boundary in his art or in his life. But I wonder if that's possible for an artist. Montaigne and Proust, most famously, withdrew from the world so they could better understand it, but unlike Gilbert they did so after a lifetime of intimate involvements. If you live only in that one dimension, how do you even know if anything exists beyond it? How could Gilbert possibly have imagined that his life was about "taking chances"? He clearly didn't know the first thing about taking chances, because he never wagered even the least portion of himself.

It's odd that I should take Jack Gilbert so personally, as if his lifestyle choices were some sort of direct challenge or insult to me. After all, maybe he was neither a hypocrite nor a poseur, but merely a flawed seeker of the truth, which would be not only forgivable but altogether admirable. Many very intelligent people admire him as both a poet and as a role model, and it is perfectly plausible that I have misinterpreted much of what he said by filtering it through a warped, defensive awareness of my own inadequacies. I mean, really, I have just written an essay's worth of vitriol against a man I have little connection to, whose life never crossed paths with my own or with the lives of anyone I know, and of whom I am in some real peril of seriously misinterpreting. What is wrong with me? I will rephrase that—why do I keep writing about other people when it's become patently obvious that I am only writing about myself? Other than the fact that this is almost the perfect definition of what novelists do, and even though I am not writing a novel here, it's a hard habit to shake.

On the one hand, it's perfectly reasonable for me to take Gilbert's condescension personally. After all, when he blithely dismisses "those people," he is talking about me, and it rightly upsets me that the boorish prejudices of a man who is widely admired, respected, and emulated should be taken at face value. What if "those people" meant "Jews" or "blacks" instead of "the bourgeois literary establishment"? The phrase would still be based on offensive, uninformed received wisdom.

Ultimately, however, it's also true—it must be true—that I get angry because I see myself in Gilbert, and Gilbert in myself. He is always going on about his rejection of the world; I am always going on about living in two worlds. Everybody knows that Jack Gilbert was a lone wolf and a trailblazer; everybody (who cares) knows that I am the novelist with a full-time job who gets up at 4:00 a.m. to write before going to his office. They praise me for my fortitude, just as they praised Gilbert for his. When I see it in someone else I find it distasteful and disingenuous, and I grow resentful that this person reminds me of myself. The hypocrisy, the emotional laziness, the self-regard—I have seen them all somewhere before, somewhere close by, and I suppose they must be easier to condemn and forgive in someone else than to recognize and repudiate in myself. Because if Jack Gilbert—a man who devoted almost his entire life to a mission that I am too timid to even broach—failed in his quest for authenticity, what chance is there for someone like me? Where is the lottery that can buy me that?

One staple of tabloid journalism nowadays is the story of people who have won the lottery, squandered their vast wealth ruinously, and returned to ignorant penury in a matter of a few brief years. It's no secret why these stories are popular. No one reads them as cautionary tales about the dangers of winning the lottery; on the contrary, they are written as fluff pieces to comfort our own sense of superiority, because, as we now know, we are always our best selves in our fantasy lives. "If I won the lottery," we tell ourselves with smug confidence, "I would know how to put it to its best use." We would husband it, invest it conservatively, make the world a better place with it, have moderate, sensible fun with it, distribute it magnanimously but thoughtfully to the deserving poor. We would appreciate our good fortune at its true value; we would make it last and we would make it count. We would definitely not be among *Business Insider*'s "13 Lottery Winners Who Lost It All," including the New Jersey woman who blew through five million dollars in Atlantic City and now lives in a trailer park, or the guy who financed the drug habit that killed his beloved granddaughter. We would be the smart ones. Likewise, when we peep in on the lives of the vulgar rich showcased on reality television, we know in our hearts that we would not spit in the face of fortune or squander our millions on trinkets and glitter like they do. We would handle our wealth with wisdom and humility because we are not the kind of people who confuse our self-worth with our bank account. We would turn that money into a force for good, and we would know how to use it in a way that made our families and ourselves happier. When I look you in the eye and tell you that my only reason for coveting that money is to buy myself the freedom to devote myself to what really matters, you are left momentarily speechless with admiration and respect because you recognize me as one of the rare breed who understand the true, occult meaning and potential of money, and are not merely dazzled by its superficial sparkle.

Of course, you don't need to win Mega Millions, or even play it, if you win the birth lottery. That's what happened to Natalie Clifford Barney, and she never had to work a day in her life. Even though we seem to be living in a new gilded age, you don't see a lot of that these days—people who don't work because they don't need the money. Maybe that's because in our puritan times most people, even the superwealthy, turn to work to give their lives meaning, and do not necessarily draw attention to the work-free aspect of their existence. Or maybe it's just that I don't know enough rich people, because the few I do know who were born rich enough not to work, work anyway. Furthermore, to the best of my knowledge, and despite the tired cliché, their wealth does not seem in any way to have made them happier than they would have been without it. The same cannot be said of Natalie Clifford Barney. "I love money," she acknowledged, "& need it for I haven't so far found a profession—nor do I see my way to becoming self supporting." When it comes to people who understand the right way to win the lottery, Natalie Barney sure seemed to be one of us.

Edith Wharton called her "something—appalling." Even as a teenager she was willful and disobedient. She rode astride and refused to wear corsets or cut her hair. She had her first affair at fifteen. In 1899, at age twenty-two, she seduced Liane de Pougy, the most famous courtesan of the Belle Époque and often described as the most beautiful woman in France. While Natalie's cruel, temperamental, controlling father was alive and she remained dependent on him, she managed to keep within the bounds of respectability, though barely. Once he died in 1902, all bets were off. By the time she was in her mid-twenties, she was already the thinly veiled lesbian heroine of novels by three celebrated Parisians. In addition to Pougy, her lovers included the poet Pauline Tarn (writing as Renée Vivien), the painter Romaine Brooks, the writer Colette, and Antoinette Corisande Élisabeth de Gramont, the Duchesse de Clermont-Tonnerre.

She led a life of unbelievable self-indulgence: luxury travel all over Europe, villas in Greece, the Orient Express, no commitments of any sort, total freedom of a kind unknown to all but a very few in this world, let alone beautiful young women. At the height of the Great Depression, she built the Villa Trait d'Union in Saint-Tropez—a "hyphenated" vacation home consisting of two separate buildings connected by a dining room—to accommodate her lover's need for solitude. She kept a riverboat for outings on the Seine. In 1909, at the age of thirty-two, she moved into a seventeenth-century pavilion on an interior courtyard in Paris's Left Bank. It had a Greek temple and a grove of trees dominated by an ancient chestnut. It was there, at 20 rue Jacob, that she lived for the next sixty years and hosted the most celebrated literary salon of the twentieth century.

Truly, Natalie Clifford Barney not only won the birth lottery but also exploited her great good fortune in precisely the way I and those like me believe we would do were we to win the lottery—she spent an entire lifetime doing exactly as she pleased, with no apparent concern for the opinions and pieties of her detractors and in a manner calculated to make an enduring statement about the rewards of keeping an open mind and remaining fully alive to life's offerings. In other words, she set out, with all the money in the world, to test exactly the same theory as Jack Gilbert, who approached the quest, very obviously, from precisely the opposite starting point.

There was, to be sure, an awful lot of money on both sides of her family. On the maternal side, she was the granddaughter of Sam Pike, who made his money in whiskey, dry goods, and real estate in Cincinnati, where he built Pike's Opera House. His beloved daughter, and the only one of his children who shared his devotion to the arts, was Natalie's mother, the renowned painter Alice Pike Barney. After the Civil War the family moved to New York, where Sam built another opera house, at Twenty-Third and Eighth. As a child and teenager, Alice traveled all over Europe and was engaged at seventeen to the British explorer Henry Morton Stanley, who pined for her in the jungles of Africa and was brokenhearted when she married Albert Clifford Barney and moved to Dayton, in her ancestral Ohio.

Albert was the son of E. E. Barney, a self-made man and the founder of Barney & Smith, the premier railcar builder in the United States. He was a nasty, conventional, snobbish drunk, and it was a bad marriage from the beginning. Even as a child, Natalie had a front-row view of what a small man can do to a willful, talented woman.

But Natalie grew up mostly in Europe, where her mother was best able to shield her from her father's cruelty. She spoke fluent French and German, was an accomplished equestrian, swimmer, fencer, and violinist, and attended the exclusive and progressive boarding school Les Ruches, in Fontaine-bleau, where girls were taught to think independently and logically. According to her biographer Suzanne Rodriguez, Natalie drew two life lessons from her early years. From her father, she learned that marriage "annihilated independence; it was stifling, debilitating. Young as she was, she knew she wanted no part of it. Not ever." From Les Ruches, she learned who she was. She

> approached this new, privileged world with a bedrock sense of entitlement. And she fit the part. At Les Ruches she'd lived in close quarters with girls who possessed great wealth and highborn titles . . . Natalie left Les Ruches feeling that membership in this ruling class was her birthright.

Natalie had no interest in going to college. Since life as a carefree heiress had few limits—and even fewer for someone who sneered at convention and social opprobrium—she wanted to get it rolling as soon as possible. She was already a voracious reader and an avid writer of poetry. Later, inspired by her friend Eva Palmer, she learned Greek so as to be closer to Sappho and the other ancient poets. Rodriguez notes that "in a sense her entire life, with its pursuit of literature and litterateurs, can be seen as a ceaseless quest for self-education." Unfortunately, her lack of a formal education seems to have had a definite downside, as she never did learn to practice disciplined thinking and work habits, and her writing, such as it was, was largely characterized as lazy throughout her career, even by her friends. Her biographer puts a philosophical spin on it, claiming that Natalie "tried hard to dispense with creative suffering altogether," but Barney herself was more candid, if less self-aware: "I never take an idea to its conclusion—that would be going too far."

Natalie's rejection of monogamy was not limited to marriage or to men. Although her affairs with a few of her lovers, and most especially Romaine Brooks, were long-lasting, they were always fraught with drama, controlling behavior by Natalie, and serial infidelities. With Pougy, Natalie wanted her all to herself, but Pougy was a professional and not willing to trust her future to one lover, howsoever wealthy, which proved very wise on her part. With Brooks, the painter was perpetually irritated by Barney's insatiable social life and her entourage of sycophants. Natalie believed that fidelity was most honored in the breach. Her need to control and dominate often seemed to make her somewhat indifferent to the suffering of lovers and friends. It is not too much of a stretch to suggest that her well-documented anti-Semitism drew its strength from the same source; if she was unable to control something or someone, including longtime friends and lovers like Eva Palmer and Pauline Tarn, she tended to dismiss them with casual cruelty.

Barney published poetry, plays, and epigrams throughout her life, but she never took to her literary vocation with the seriousness that we usually associate with a professional writer. Although it has its moments of wit and sharp aperçus, her best-known work, *Pensées d'une amazone*, a collection of aphorisms and curtailed political musings, reads today like the kind of point-of-purchase compendium you find in the bathrooms of hip literati. Even her dear friend Ezra Pound wrote in *The Dial*: "Natalie Barney . . . has published with complete mental laziness a book of unfinished sentences and broken paragraphs."

She is essentially unreadable. Every sentence is an aphorism, even when she is not writing aphorism but portraits, as if she were telling her readers, her critics, and herself: "See? Every word I write is quotable!" She is like an orator whose speeches consist of nothing but climaxes and conclusions. No discipline, no editorial control, no self-censorship. Her adages are all polish, no substance. Her literary references are myriad and often willfully obscure, as if she were goading people into comparing her to Montaigne. I hate to say it, but in her writing she comes across as a smug little rich girl who is very pleased with herself and will never have to answer for her failure to complete anything.

In 1910, Barney met and befriended the writer and critic

Rémy de Gourmont, who had become a recluse after being disfigured by lupus. Whether or not it is true that Natalie's "conquest" of Gourmont was mercenary or "cold-blooded," as many seemed to think, it had the desired effect. It was Gourmont who, in his *Lettres à l'Amazone*, gave her the epithet that she was to bear proudly for the rest of her life. Once she was able to stride out into the literary world as Gourmont's Amazon, nothing could stop her.

Suzanne Rodriguez, referring to Barney's "vague desire to ally herself with artists and creativity," suggests that she launched her salon out of the misfit's need to fit in somewhere and feel comfortable, but to me it seems pretty clear that she wanted to put herself in a position in which she could be surrounded by admiring literary elites without having to try too hard to be one of them. It reinforced her sense of her rightful place in the world. Her friend Lucie Delarue-Mardrus describes her salon:

> . . . her magnetic force also attracts only celebrities, while the quiet vigor with which she hates mediocrity repels from her entourage everything which, even from afar, borders on banality . . . In the middle of this dense crowd, which is gathered around her charm, is Natalie. Dressed in white, wrapped in some ermine capes, smiling and detached, she lets each one interpret her in his own fashion.

As Rodriguez says, "Natalie had been in training her entire life to take on this role." Regulars to her salon included Rabindranath Tagore, Rainer Maria Rilke, Paul Valéry, Ezra Pound, Ford Madox Ford, Ernest Hemingway, Colette,

André Gide, Pierre Louÿs, Anatole France, Paul Claudel, Max Jacob, Louis Aragon, Jean Cocteau, Janet Flanner, Mina Loy, Djuna Barnes. Even Gertrude Stein—the doyenne of the far more *moderne* salon only a mile away and someone who took her own literary talents very seriously indeed—was eventually won over. Although Barney's salon was perceived as rather staid and elitist following the Great War and the advent of the Jazz Age, especially as compared with Stein's, Natalie Barney is rightly considered to this day to have been the hostess of one of the great literary salons of twentieth-century Europe.

Let's go back a minute to the idea that we are our best selves in our parallel lives, the ones we did not get to live. Natalie Barney's charmed life was, obviously, not her fantasy life; it was the real thing, and it's clear that no matter how well your life has turned out, or even if you are handed the golden ticket on the day of your birth, you are still entitled to a fantasy life in which everything is different. Nevertheless, in most ways Natalie Barney made it clear that she was living life very close to the border between mundane reality and idealized fantasy. When she wrote "Entertained by everything, concerned by nothing: freedom," she was referring not to some unattainable platonic ideal of freedom, but to her own life and her own self. Aphorism as self-portrait. Likewise with "Equality is an inferior status." And when she writes "This mania for owning things astounds me—what wisdom it is to own nothing," she is laying out a vision of the world that can be seen only through the eyes of the person who has everything. And yet, it is very clear that Barney, like Jack Gilbert, never really came very close to becoming the best version of herself.

"Little by little, as the years passed," writes Rodriguez, "Natalie would harden her heart and narrow her vision until only the inhabitants of her circle held reality. The world at large would come to have little meaning for Natalie Clifford Barney." "I am fond of human beings," Barney noted in *Pensees d'une amazone*, "but only one at a time." She harbored absolutely no sense of solidarity with or loyalty to women in general—she characterized mothers as "virgins nostalgic for a love they have never known"—and her fellow feminists in particular: "English women are by necessity militant; they gain their women's rights by sacrificing all the effects of femininity."

In her book *Adventures of the Mind*, she enlisted many of her close friends to write essays about her. Many, of course, are flattering verging on sycophantic, but even those cannot entirely restrain the restless truth lying just below the surface. She is described as the embodiment of "flamboyant self-aggrandizement" and as "obstinate and obsessing." "She can upbraid you for hours, without anyone understanding anything, for some very little thing that has displeased her; or else insist, likewise for hours, on forcing you to do the opposite of what has been decided." Despite her wealth, her idea of helping her penurious literary friends Paul Valéry and T. S. Eliot was not to subsidize them but to sell shares in them—thirty shares per writer at five hundred francs apiece, for a total of thirty thousand francs. Derek Patmore wrote of her "direct, penetrating and absolutely pitiless gaze" and of "the ruthlessness beneath the smooth surface of the clever, well-bred wealthy American who long ago had decided to conquer

Europe." Pauline Tarn told her that she had "charm and grace, but more often you are imperious and despite yourself you do bad things." And when her former lover Eva Palmer fell in love with someone else (a man!) and Natalie was unable to express any happiness for her, Palmer responded with the unvarnished truth about the life Barney had created for herself in the midst of her entourage: "The same tiresome little people you brought me to, the same eternal little intrigues and passions you chose to live among when you had me to mold as you chose. We were both as free as the wind, we might have gone to any beautiful place and done any noble thing . . . I am tired of you and all the little things you care for."

In the end, of course, we don't judge Barney for not being a nice person, or for spending her wealth as she saw fit. We judge her for being a careless, lazy writer and a mediocre poet, for treating literature the way she treated her own freedom, without thought for the outcome, because she could afford, financially and emotionally, to ignore the fallout. She approached writing the same way she approached her lovers— deep momentary passion followed by relative indifference. "I am not miserly with those who can do without me," she wrote, "nor with those whom I manage to do without." Just like Jack Gilbert, she had absolutely no interest in what anyone else was doing, feeling, or thinking.

No matter how you might feel about them, both Barney and Gilbert seem to have achieved precisely what they set out to achieve and to have lived precisely as they set out to live. Is it a coincidence that they were both so unlikable? Is it in the nature of people who are able to get what they want to be unsympathetic and impervious to the opinions of others, or is it the fact that they get exactly what they want that makes them that way? Or is it simply the envy and incomprehension of those who have failed to do what they succeeded in doing that places them in an unfavorable light? I had set out to identify a role model in someone who, unlike me, had found a way by good fortune or sheer resolve to live life precisely as he or she chose. This is no easy matter, as very few of us do, and many of us may toy with the idea that we would be both happier and better people if we did. I found two people who seemed to have done just that, and although I approached these subjects with compassion and an open heart, I found myself repelled by both of them. I am not by inclination a fault-finder; I certainly didn't go out with the intention of finding two perfect strangers, admired and beloved by many who knew them, so that I could trash their characters and set myself up as their moral superior. So what is going on here?

I would like to think that the dynamic at work is the one encapsulated in the formulation "be careful what you wish for"—that somehow there is a curse attached to getting exactly what you want. The curse could be psychological, evolutionary, genetic, sociocultural, but whatever you might choose to ascribe it to, it is an ineluctable component of human nature. If you win the lottery, you will be punished. It is, of course, a very ancient perspective, which is why it's known by an assortment of Greek terms, but it doesn't work in this case unless you believe that being an insufferable narcissist is a cause of suffering to the narcissist himself, even if he is wholly unaware of how other people perceive him. While it may seem to me that Jack Gilbert cannot possibly be happy as a person who is interested only in his own happiness, Jack probably did not see it that way. Likewise, I don't think Natalie Barney suffered pangs of regret or a sense of inferiority every time someone flattered her shamelessly, or every time she thoughtlessly scolded her friends and her servants. In other words, if you feel quite secure in the La-Z-Boy of your own ego, you are less likely to consider that you have been spoiled by having it all—in fact, essentially ruined as a creature with potential for empathy and selflessness—and if it does, the realization will amuse rather than pain you.

Another possible, and more plausible, explanation is that it is not your good fortune that has cut you off, but that good fortune happens only to the right kind of person. Jack Gilbert had always been the way he was at eighty, and it was being that sort of person that won him the lottery. Likewise, Natalie Barney being the person she was, she would have found a way to be the center of attention no matter what social class she had been born into. It is not the environment that creates the narcissist; it is the narcissist who creates the environment in which she can thrive.

Then, of course, there's always the possibility that I have hinted at before, namely, that it is all in my imagination. In this light, Jack and Natalie were perfectly charming, considerate, generous souls, curious about everything and everyone and eager to connect at a deeply emotional level with other people's experience; it is simply me, stewing in envy at the opportunities that life afforded them but denied me, who sees them through the warped telescope of my own inadequacies.

I have maligned them out of jealousy and spite because they have escaped all the traps that tether me to the earth. That is a possibility, as far as it goes. I suppose I can be as envious as the next man, and it's never very pretty when I catch myself at it. But it's a very limited direction of inquiry, because it doesn't explain why I would be searching for role models who inspire my contempt.

I think finally that the dialectic at work with me and my subjects is that, ultimately, I am always projecting myself into my portraits of others. I think that, deep down, I do not fully believe in myself as the kind of person who would not be ruined by winning the lottery; in fact, I suspect that I am just the kind of weak-willed mediocrity who would let it all go to his head and make the worst possible use of his good fortune. So when I look at Jack and Natalie, and I am angered by their smugness and their blindness and their egotism, I am only seeing them ape my failings back at me in a form that I cannot deny, since it's my own projection. That is not only why I take their shortcomings and foibles so personally, but also why I chose them as role models to begin with. I was not looking for someone who could model the honest lottery-winner for me; I was looking for someone who could show me as I really am, and as I suspect I really would be, were I to find myself in their shoes. I would not be the guy who wakes up every day with a paean of gratitude on my lips; I'd be the guy who thought he had pulled a fast one on the humble, ignorant masses. I would not be the Montaigne who wisely used the freedom offered by his wealth to retire in philosophical contemplation; I would be the F. Scott Fitzgerald who cast his pearls before swine and drank himself into an early grave, never fully convinced that anything I had ever produced had any intrinsic value whatsoever. It's my way of telling myself, "Get real. Did you really think that winning the lottery would help you be the man or the writer you always thought you could be if you hadn't had to work so hard all your life? You're fifty-two years old. Do you think *anything* could help you change at this point, if you haven't done it for yourself already?"

Hunger Artists

I'm not a big follower of sports, but a recent article in the *New York Times Magazine* caught my attention. Written by Jonathan Mahler, "The Coach Who Exploded" explores the career of Mike Rice, a well-known basketball coach at Rutgers University who was fired and disgraced for his abusive treatment of his players. The article also follows Rice in the aftermath of the scandal as he tries to redeem himself, not professionally but morally, with the help of a "rehabilitation coach" named John Lucas, who tells him that one critical lesson on the road to redemption is that he will have to learn that he's just another "bozo on the bus." What Lucas means by this, I believe, is that Rice, whose career in a brutally competitive profession was played out in the national public eye, will have to get used to the idea that from now on he is a nobody. There is nothing special about him; he is no longer rich or famous and is unlikely to be either in the future; people will never again defer to him because of his status; and he can never again consider himself unbound by the rules that govern the common standards of behavior, respect, and consideration that apply to the rest of us. It is only once Rice has recognized, internalized, and accepted his new position as a zero, a common man in the broadest sense of the term, that he can truly begin to reconstruct his sense of himself in the world and to move forward again, hopefully, toward some kind of serenity and happiness. According to Mahler, Rice seems to have endorsed this prognosis and is working in dogged humility to that end.

I should imagine that the reason I was drawn to this article, on a subject in which I would otherwise have little interest, would be pretty evident. I would like to say that there is an ugly secret shared among writers and artists, but I can't pretend that I know anything about what goes on in the hearts of other writers, so instead I will say that I harbor an ugly secret. I'm not sure what makes it ugly, or rather what makes me think it's ugly, but I do nevertheless. Maybe "ugly" isn't even the right word; perhaps "dirty" or "shameful" or "embarrassing" are closer to the truth. And this ugly, dirty, shameful, and/or embarrassing truth is that I wish I were famous—a famous writer. We are not supposed to go into the arts for fame or money; we are supposed to do it because something inside us compels us to. And indeed, that's true for most of us, I imagine, because there are so many easier ways to become famous than by struggling in a crowded field whose highest rewards and honors are, at best, a matter of indifference to the vast majority of the world's peoples. If you're interested in being famous just for the sake of it, you'd have to be a moron trying to do it in my line of work. I know that as well as the next person, and I would be a moron myself—doing what I do and knowing what I know about the paltry significance attached to literary fiction by our culture—to go on in the same vein in the forlorn hope of winning fame and fortune. I do it for any number of reasons, most of which I cannot fathom and some of which don't even qualify as "reasons," but one of them, believe it or not, is so that one day I can walk into a bookstore anywhere in the country and be recognized, or that I will see someone reading my book on the subway and that person will look up and smile at me. Or that I will be honored by my peers with a prestigious award and asked to give an acceptance speech before the elite in my chosen field. I want to be admired and remembered by strangers, and I haven't the faintest idea why I do or should. If you're an actor, an athlete, or a politician, say, there doesn't seem to be anything wrong with wanting to be famous; indeed, it's hard to imagine getting ahead in those impossible fields without that kind of focus and drive. For me, though, it just feels wrong—weak, vain, and ignorant—but it's part of who I am. I know—I am absolutely certain—that it's possible for most people to lead the happiest, most fulfilling lives being loved and admired by their family and friends alone, and even that it ought to be every righteous person's highest, most cherished goal to be thought of as kind, wise, generous, and gentle by those who know him. What could it possibly matter if I should die unknown and unsung except by those who know and love me? Still, unlike Mike Rice, I cannot and will not accept the fact that I am just another bozo on the bus.

It might be worth exploring what we mean, or rather what I mean, when I talk about "success." On the face of it, that ought to be relatively easy. If you're an athlete and you win competitions, you're a success. If you're a politician and you win elections, you're a success. If you go into business to make money, and if you make money, you're a success. You manage a profitable startup and you're a success. You run a large bank and manage to stay out of jail, and you're a success. But even as a businessman your definition of success will usually include some kind of happiness. Most people won't think of themselves as successful if they're as lonely and unloved as Scrooge. So, being successful as a businessman immediately becomes more complicated than making as much money as one can. Even someone who goes into a business without any particular passion for the product he's selling is compelled to view his success through a larger lens because he's only human. Although I'm sure there are plenty of CEOs who don't give a shit about family or being liked (rather than feared or envied), I doubt that's true of 99 percent of them—although I say that without actually knowing any CEOs.

For artists, this confusion is multiplied by multiple factors. When Vladimir Nabokov died, Donald Barthelme wrote to Joyce Carol Oates: "Nabokov died yesterday, we all move up a notch." It was a joke, of course, but it pinpoints the problem of ambition as experienced, or endured, by artists. Nobody moves up anywhere when someone else dies; there's no hierarchy except the one you imagine in your head: "I wish I were as famous as X. I wish I were as respected by my peers as Y." I would venture to say that most writers of any kind, even genre authors who crank out a book a year as if they were building lawn mowers, couldn't define what they mean by "success," and that there are plenty of "successful" folk out there who think of themselves as anything but. I know at least one writer who had a nervous breakdown when he made the transition from comparative obscurity, beloved by a small but selective audience, to bestseller. He had worked so hard to convince himself that his work was too smart and literary for the masses that when he looked in the mirror after his break-through, he experienced a kind of creative dysmorphia—his wonderful new popularity, fully merited as it was, seemed like a kind of failure. People have been making art for twenty thousand years, at a bare minimum, and nobody anywhere, at any time, has been able to figure out why we do it or what it means. In that context, a nervous breakdown seems like a perfectly reasonable response to his predicament.

In July 2013, Dwight Garner reviewed the collected short stories of James Purdy for the *New York Times*. Although he published dozens of novels, short story collections, and plays; although Gore Vidal called him "an authentic American ge-nius"; and although his works were translated into more than thirty languages, in his own lifetime and today Purdy was and remains a marginal literary figure. This may be because, in an age of conformity, his subject matter was ahead of its time, his style considered cutting-edge, his characters outsiders. Garner was not impressed. He wrote: "If I'm not persuaded [of Purdy's genius], Purdy, to his credit, would scarcely have cared. 'I don't think I'd like it if people liked me,' he once said. 'I'd think something had gone wrong.'"

First, can anyone really believe a writer who claims not to care if anyone likes his work? If you don't write for other people to read, why do you write? Is it purely exorcism, or purgative? That does not make art, it makes diaries, and Purdy was anything but a diarist. His defiance of other people's opinions rings as defensive and hurt, as if he had spent a lifetime building up his defenses against the world's relative indifference. I certainly can't judge him for that, but on the basis of that one assertion I would say it was patently untrue that he didn't care.

Secondly, he says "if people like me," not "if people like my work." That shows confused thinking, which is also probably widespread among artists. In my world, I am completely muddled with my work—if someone doesn't like my work I find it hard to understand how they could like me. Of course I take it personally. I suspect that Purdy felt the same way, so he threw out the baby with the bathwater. "I don't care if you don't like me or my work. In fact, there is something wrong with me, so if you like me or my work there must be something wrong with you." So don't ask yourself whether you want to be loved by your loved ones or admired by strangers. It's the wrong question. You have to ask yourself instead: Is there something inherently unhealthy, neurotic, or spiritually bereft about my ambition? If you answered yes, then ask yourself this: Is that a question you would have asked yourself if you considered yourself to be successful?

At the age of fifty or thereabouts, a lot of us are not where we want to be, or at least not where we once thought we would want to be by this time in our lives—professionally, emotionally, spiritually, artistically, or philosophically—whatever our ambitions for ourselves once entailed. This isn't necessarily about money or professional success; perhaps we thought advancing age would make us or help us to be more mature, or more generous, or more tolerant, or more truthful, or more serene, but it hasn't. Most of us get past this disappointment by joking about lowered expectations, and even if it hurts to say it out loud, it's a wise thing to take lightly, because the fact is that success of any kind, in any arena, is by its very nature a rarity. If more people succeeded at what they do than failed, the very nature of success would be altered, because it would no longer enjoy the elite cachet that makes it desirable. To put it at its crudest, if success is to have any meaning, more people have to lose than win. That is true even if your idea of success is abstract in the extreme. The spectrum of success for a writer, for instance, can range from composing the perfect quatrain that few but her peers will ever read, to making millions churning out romance or thriller series. A chef can aspire equally to prepare the perfect roast chicken or to found an international archipelago of branded restaurants. A businessman can be optimally successful keeping his family hardware store relevant and afloat for another generation, or running a hedge fund worth tens of billions of dollars. I take it as given that it is just as difficult to succeed at quatrains, roast chicken, and hardware as at anything else, so the truth remains that it is inevitable that most people will not succeed, or succeed to their own satisfaction, at whatever it is they turn their hand to.

As a result, not caring to define ourselves exclusively as the sum total of our achievements, and hoping without much empirical proof that there is an inner core within us that remains constant and independent—like the molten heart of a planet that churns on regardless of what mountain ranges, oceans, or tropical forests cling to the surface—most of us learn to live with and make light of our disappointments. We tell ourselves precisely this: that many, many people—the vast majority, in fact—are able to go on to lead happy, balanced, productive lives after they have faced and accepted the reality that their dreams are not likely to come true and that clinging to their frustrated ambitions is ultimately a self-defeating and fruitless martyrdom. We strive to persuade ourselves that who we are is separate and distinct from what we have achieved, even though we have been schooled since birth to understand that that is not how the world works, since every single protagonist on the world stage who has made it into the history books or the literary cannon, or onto the walls of the great museums, or has had a dinosaur or a hospital or a hedge fund or a peninsula or a weapon named after her, has done so on the basis of her achievements and, more important still, of her *success* in getting the world to recognize those achievements. It's hard work, letting go of all that, dissociating our *selves* from our work and our status, and many of us are only partially successful at it, but it's the wise thing to do if we want to be happyish, and most of us can get it right to a certain extent. Many of us never wanted that much to begin with—or at least, never wanted *it all*—and maybe it's a little easier that way, but surely almost all of us have wanted at one time or another to hang some tinselly achievement great or small to the Christmas tree of our identity, and have failed in our attempts to do so. It shouldn't be a big deal, since it's such a common, uniting experience, yet it usually is. We can't even bear to picture our maidenly egos alone in the room with the lecher Failure, let alone see them wedded to one another, but we have to learn to live with it if we don't wish to walk around exuding the acrid stench of bitterness.

Artists in general have a default mode for such resignation that should be the envy of all who strive. If you're successful in business, you probably love what you do, which is very important, but it's hard to deny that the primary yardstick for measuring your success is how much money you make. Yet if you're a musician, a painter, or most especially a poet, you can say "I'm not in it for the money" with a kind of offhand self-deprecation that most people will find perfectly convincing. If a poet were to tell you that he was in it for the money, you might believe him but you'd think he was delusional. Indeed, art—like medicine and politics—is one of the few realms of human endeavor in which there is something a little unseemly about claiming a motive of pure profit. Artists are expected to be in it for something other than the money, and those few who make a virtue of being openly mercenary tend not to be taken very seriously by their peers or their public.

In his book *The Gift*—highly beloved by artists, most especially the struggling ones, in all fields—Lewis Hyde demonstrates very convincingly that something cannot be called a work of art at all unless it partakes of the gift economy. He defines a gift as something that, like a work of art, has value only as an item of exchange, increases in value with the exchange, and loses all value when hoarded. The artist's "gift" is that which he receives from the universe, for lack of a better word; he increases it through his labor, then increases it again by passing it on, like DNA. His gift has no value if it is not shared, but it becomes a living thing when it is; the artist feeds and channels life itself, the noblest goal of all, so long as he always treats the fruits of the imagination as a gift and not a commodity. *The Gift* is a complex and moving meditation, and I do not do it justice by summarizing it. It is not aimed exclusively at artists, but artists tend to gravitate to it as one of the few coherent and integral attempts to make sense of their place in a capitalist society, without either hand-wringing pathos or false snobbery about their elevated mission. Although written in the 1980s, *The Gift* is to the twenty-first century what Rilke's *Letters to a Young Poet* was to the twentieth—a must-read for any young person considering a life in the arts.

At the same time, of all the blurbs the book's publishers could have put on its front cover, they chose this by Margaret Atwood: "The best book I know of for talented but unacknowledged creators." In other words, the publisher seems to believe that the book's primary audience is not those who seek guidance, wisdom, or exaltation, but artists who need to be comforted for their failure to make the world recognize their gift. Even Atwood, who is highly acknowledged and in no need of comfort, seems to believe that the main thrust of *The Gift* is to make us feel good about ourselves when the world remains indifferent to our talents. That's not how I read the book, and I am almost positive it's not how Hyde intended it, but it obviously sells product, since it appeals to the 99 percent of us who are trying to make sense of why we are not appreciated by strangers at our due worth.

The point is that artists, more than almost any other social class, are expected to find their primary satisfaction in simply doing their work, rather than in any ancillary reward such as fame, money, or power. The fact that none of these is readily available to most artists is not expected to stand in their way, as it might if they were Wall Street analysts or orthodontists. If you go into business selling insurance, you remain a businessperson even if you go into some other profit-making venture that might suit you better or be more profitable. But an artist who quits making art because there's no money in it is rightly considered to be an artist no longer, and was probably never one to begin with. An artist has a legitimate right to make his fortune and reputation through his work, but that is not allowed to be his primary consideration. If it is, he is doing something a little different than making art; he is manufacturing a commercial product for sale whose market value is determined by its capacity to vaguely resemble a work of art without actually being one, much the way the value of a semiautomatic rifle on the civilian market is based on its resemblance to a military assault weapon.

This is where the distinction arises between the notion of success and the notion of fulfillment. Success is a social construct, whereas fulfillment is purely personal: how you act or feel around others versus how you act or feel when you are alone. Someone else can tell you whether or not you are a success, whereas no one but you knows if you are fulfilled. To be or to feel successful is to see yourself as others see you; to be fulfilled is in itself a feeling—a GPS satellite with itself as its sole coordinate—with no objective benchmarks and no susceptibility to external influence. A self-made millionaire can be made to feel a failure by the billionaire next door, but no one who is fulfilled can be brought low by someone else's happiness.

Most of us start out as callow youths thinking that what we seek is success, and end up—if we're very wise and very lucky—settling for fulfillment. But the artist is supposed from the very outset to be searching for fulfillment in his work—which presumably derives from a hard-won confluence of his inchoate attraction to a platonic vision and his talent to make that vision material to his own satisfaction—and not worldly success, which allows others to assign a worth to your achievement. The problem, of course, is that hardly any of us can be fully confident of knowing on which side of the divide we stand.

In the documentary film *Jiro Dreams of Sushi*, the world-famous eighty-five-year-old Tokyo sushi chef Jiro Ono and his two sons repeatedly insist that they do not do what they do for the money, and you never doubt that they are telling the truth, but they have a much harder time explaining what they *are* doing it for, other than reaching for some transcendent, otherworldly ideal of what sushi can be. There's no question that the film is a portrait of the artist as an old man at the top of his game; I'm not trying to compare sushi to the work of Beethoven or Dante or Michelangelo, but Ono's rather inarticulate yet supremely confident definition of what drives him is as proximate as any I know to what drives many artists. You're not doing it for money, because there often is little or none to be had; you're not exactly doing it for pleasure, since the things you may need are not always the things you enjoy or even want; you'd be a fool to do it for glory, though many of us do nonetheless; perhaps you do it for release or catharsis or healing, but I don't think that could be factored into a comprehensive definition. The closest I can come to it is to say, clumsily, that you serve it in the manner and the spirit of a medieval vassal serving his liege lord—both because you need to do it, but also because you do not doubt that you were born to serve and that the universal order is somehow appeased and upheld when you do so competently and willingly. As a feudal peon you sincerely believed that it was God's will that you accept your place in the order of the world, and that in fulfilling your obligation you were doing what pleased Him best, because even the mightiest prince was still but a lowly servant to the Almighty. An artist derives a similar satisfaction and peace from humbly serving her art—not practicing but *serving*—and accepting and asserting her place in the universe by doing so. She may never get there—she may never attain the serenity of the believer who has learned to put all her faith in God and leave all the worrying to Him—but that is the mountain she's trying to climb, whether she knows it or not. You do it because you need to do it, because you are *commanded* to do it, and you can only hope and pray that in return it will give you what you need, even if you have no idea what that might be, other than some nebulous principle of fulfillment.

An artist's apprenticeship can seem eternal, thankless, and full of drudgery. Jiro Ono's apprentices spend ten years learning to bake eggs before they're even allowed to touch the fish; a young writer or painter can expect a similar wait for the first meager payoff. But what if you go through all of that and it still doesn't give you what you need, or even help you to understand what it is you need? What if you were to enter a strict monastic order of enforced poverty, silence, and seclusion, with no expectation of eventual release, and once there you were to pray to God every day, and after twenty, thirty, or forty years you were still no more convinced that he has heard you, or that he even exists, than you were on the day you started? The day must come when you are forced to ask yourself what it's all been for, and why you've spent your entire life on such an elusive quest. In fact, you cannot even hope to enjoy grace and enlightenment until every last ember of hope and faith has been thoroughly doused. Almost all of us who have ever sat down to write a book or a poem, or make a film, or build a business or a career, will reach that crossroads at one point or another. The question doesn't have to be existential, in the sense that Sartre or Camus would read it—"Why should I not kill myself?"—but it should at the very least prompt us to stop whatever we are doing at the moment and sit down in front of a mirror and ask ourselves, slowly, directly, and in deadly earnest: What is it that I am actually looking for? What is it that I really need?

Franz Kafka was a Czech Jewish writer who died of tuberculosis in 1924. Elliott Smith was an American indie songwriter and musician who committed suicide in 2003 by stabbing himself—twice—through the heart. Other than the fact that they were both geniuses in their respective fields, the only thing they had in common, to my knowledge, was that they both spent a great deal of time, energy, and intellectual capital considering the question "What is it that I really need?" Unfortunately, for the personal happiness of both, it was the wrong question to ask. What they should have asked instead was: What is the difference between what I think I need and what I really need, and how do I tell them apart?

In his short story "A Hunger Artist," Kafka writes about a great artist who attracts vast crowds on his tours of the European capitals, where he sits in a cage and submits to the scrutiny of the prurient as he slowly starves himself over the course of weeks. The hunger artist loves to be stared at—his is an art that is consumed in the sharing—but he is convinced that few if any of his admirers truly appreciate the depth of his art. "The hunger artist was the only . . . spectator capable of being completely satisfied with his own fasting." His frustration is compounded by the time limits that his manager, not wishing to endanger the artist's life or risk losing his meal ticket, imposes on the duration of his fasts. The result is that his fasts are always cut short just as they begin to get interesting—not that his vulgar audience can tell the difference. The hunger artist would prefer not to feel contempt for his public. He would genuinely welcome the rare viewer who truly understood what he was reaching for, yet he can't help feeling that he will never be able to truly express himself, or to carry his art to its ultimate fruition, until he is free of these commercial restraints. Over the years, his art form gradually falls out of fashion, he is abandoned by his impresario, and he is reduced to performing in a traveling circus, his cage shunted to the back lot, where he is rarely noticed by the crowds hurrying past. And yet it is here, unencumbered from having to play to the crowd and from having to limit his scope of self-expression, that he finds that he is able to finally put himself to the test—to discover once and for all whether he is truly the great artist he has always believed himself to be. Unseen and unappreciated, he fasts to the furthest extreme; it is only when he is upon the very brink of death, too late to pull back, that he sees the truth about himself—that the only reason he has been a hunger artist his entire life is that he has never found anything he wanted to eat; if he had, he would have been no different from anyone else—just an ordinary, happy person without ambition.

Kafka packs an enormous amount of luggage into the one fragile valise of this short story. The persona of the hunger artist is embodiment and apotheosis of the myth of the romantic artist as outcast, indifferent to fame and fortune, and isolated by his own genius. It was a myth that would not be fully enshrined until the legend of Kafka himself—including his early, tragic death in obscurity—became the overriding template for the twentieth-century artist's life. And the template is hardly limited to artists—any angst-ridden American teenager, convinced that no one can understand her and that she is elevated into lofty inaccessibility by the epic magnificence of her emotional life, will see and recognize herself in the person of the hunger artist. You can't overstate the power of the story—both the short story and the story of Kafka's life—to encapsulate something completely essential about the Western psyche in the twentieth century. It is both something that we all understand, even if we do not see it as applying to ourselves, and a status—that of exalted, maligned genius—that many aspire to despite its perfectly obvious implications for personal happiness and fulfillment. The flip side of the Kafka-artist model is that of Einstein—the affable, gregarious, socially engaged scientist who wears his genius lightly and carelessly—but for most people there is more percentage in casting yourself as a lone, misunderstood artist than as an absentminded professor. It's an easier role to play—you have less to prove, for one thing, especially to yourself.

Elliott Smith most definitely and explicitly identified himself with the hunger artist—grotesque and difficult to look at, a freak of a certain phenotype, an artist whose true value is beyond the understanding of most people. Both have contempt for the vulgar masses who are unable to understand the elemental simplicity of their art. Both are the objects of suspicion as cheats or frauds by those who do not understand them. Both are prevented by mercenary management from taking their art to its true fruition. Smith, too, embodies the full ethos of the outsider artist in the guise of indie rocker—in it not for money or for fame but for the kind of glory that only he and a handful of others can appreciate, and with only a tiny core elite of true followers. It's a status that is very difficult to maintain in the face of broadening public acceptance, because it's based on the understanding that only an inner circle of enlightened initiates can recognize the artist's gifts. If that inner circle is overrun by a mass of undifferentiated consumers, the indie musician is put in the impossible position of either having to renounce the cult status he once embraced, and the aura of rare sensibility it had conferred on him and his fans alike, or having to reject his newfound celebrity and the second-class adulation of his wider, uninitiated audience. As we have seen again and again, a lot of musicians are unable to square that circle; some die trying. And of course, just as the popularity of hunger artists eventually waned, the popularity of all musicians, especially indies, is usually short-lived. It so happens that, on his right bicep, Smith bore a tattoo of Ferdinand the bull, whom he claimed to revere as a representative of those whom the world regards as failures because they work "outside the system," but Smith must have known that this is precisely why Ferdinand is a hero to millions—a hunger artist for toddlers. As Kafka's hunger artist discovered, it is much easier to be a hunger artist before the world calls on you to live up to your convictions.

Smith was a genius, without a doubt, in my opinion one of the greatest songwriters since the Lennon-McCartney team, to which he paid repeated tribute in his songs. He played most of the instruments on the six albums he released as a solo artist during his lifetime. I am no music critic, but if you don't know his music you should, although my wife and daughters now refuse to allow me to play it in the car because they find it relentlessly depressing, which I guess it is, on the whole.

There's a video on YouTube, dating back to the year 2000, three years before his death, in which Smith is a guest on an MTV pilot for the doomed *Jon Brion Show*, directed by Paul Thomas Anderson. The video showcases all of Smith's transcendent talents as a singer, musician, and composer. It is also a kind of window into the racked, writhing soul of precisely the kind of romantic-tragic artist sketched by Kafka in his short story.

One of the first things almost every commentator noted about Smith was his oily hair, which is in full evidence in the video, along with the terrible haircut that usually went along with it. This may seem like a trivial or even a petty focus, but the very conspicuous lack of preoccupation with his appearance, even as his fame and recognition skyrocketed, was a key element of his persona, as it was with his immediate contemporary Kurt Cobain, with whom he was often compared. I'm not suggesting that his indifference to his appearance was an affectation—on the contrary, it was clearly a genuine and intrinsic facet of his personality. Smith was not a hipster trying to be casual or grungy. Either he genuinely had no idea what he was wearing, or else he had, improbably, chosen the best clothes in his closet.

In the video, he is completely absent. No banter, no sense of humor, no sense of anyone else in the room. He is an insecure guy waiting for the first glimpse of a blind date in a restaurant that is too fancy for him. His "date" is the song he's about to play. When it starts, it's just him and her. He's trying to woo her, but he's a nerd, he's tongue-tied. He puts his all into proving himself worthy of his own song, and he seems to believe he's failed every time. At one moment, after the other musicians have laughed about their mistakes, he says very belatedly: "I think I played one bad note." Not laughing, almost nauseated with anxiety. He is completely oblivious to everyone else in the room; for him, there are no other musicians, no cameramen, no technicians, no audience. Just Elliott and the pain he has invested in his songs. Each one is vital, precious, unique, but none can save him. When he smiles at the end of a song, it is not an acknowledgment of the audience's applause—it is relief that the song has allowed him to survive its performance. When Jon Brion tries to make lighthearted banter, Smith grows supremely uncomfortable, drinks beer, and looks deeply constipated. At one point, as Smith suddenly switches from guitar to piano for "Everything Means Nothing to Me," the camera catches Brion behind his shoulder, looking as if he were about to evaporate in the shadow of Smith's genius. When it's over, Smith turns around and whispers in his ear, obviously apologizing that the song sounded like shit, completely unaware that he is on national television. Brion is game: "I didn't mind it. You want to move on to something else or do it again?" ES: "Whatever you want to do?" JB: "I thought it was pretty good, personally. I say we move on" (trying to save his doomed pilot). "I don't know if it makes you feel any better, but I messed up plenty too . . . How's everybody feeling?" There's some desperate whooping from the audience, but clearly Smith is bringing them down big-time. Finally, Brion begins to make fun of Smith for being such a lousy stage presence. Smith, laughing a little bit at himself, says, "So this is turning into an interview now?" For him, clearly, his only value is as the negligible escort to the song he's bringing to the party. He has nothing whatsoever to say for himself; he's nothing, except that this gorgeous chick he's with couldn't get in without him. Smith literally runs off the stage the moment he is done. When it comes to hunger artists, Smith was the real thing.

A couple of years earlier, in 1998, Smith had flirted even more intimately with disaster when a song he had written for Gus Van Sant's movie *Good Will Hunting* was nominated for an Academy Award. Although far from a household name, Smith had by that time already put out several albums that had been successful by indie standards, but the songs he wrote for *Good Will Hunting* and his Oscar nomination changed everything. Suddenly, uncannily, he was famous. As I said, it is inimical to all the hunger artist stands for to enjoy broad-based popular success. If you've spent your entire life convincing yourself that no one can or will ever understand you, and that popular acclaim is born of mediocrity, how are you to handle it when it comes your way? Many will make the adjustment fairly quickly and painlessly, allowing that perhaps they were not quite so success-averse as they had thought, but not Smith. He was like a deer in the headlights of celebrity. His first reaction was to refuse to go on, but he was told unequivocally that if he did not perform his song at the Oscars someone else would do it for him. He made his woebegone television network debut on *Late Night with Conan O'Brien*, and a few nights later donned a shiny white jacket and played "Miss Misery" with syrupy violins and Irish flutes at the Oscars—somehow managing to appear even more lonely and miserable than he had on *Conan*. That experience launched the decline into depression and drug abuse that culminated in his suicide five years later. He inaugurated it by signing with DreamWorks Records, a label partly owned by David Geffen, who had made big stars of the bands Nirvana and Sonic Youth. It was not an auspicious move for someone who identified as closely with his outsider status as Smith did. The artist Marc Swanson, who had been friends with Smith since their student days at Hampshire College, summarized his quandary pretty well. "It's almost like the sadness came on stronger when he started to do better . . . I was always really nervous for him because it seemed like the better he was doing, the more he had to justify to other people that he wasn't doing well . . . In one way, if you're sad, and then you have everything that's supposed to make your life good and you're still sad . . . what do you strive for after that?" It was, to be sure, not a straight line, and it was further complicated by the fact that he had frequently written about drug abuse long before he became a full-blown addict—mostly, it would seem, because the mantle of the addicted musician, whether honestly assumed or not, is often a very good fit for any hunger artist. "I'm going to do my record and I'm going to do as many drugs as I want," he told one journalist, "because art is not about being sober and it's not about being some society figure, it's about art."

Suicide would seem to be the act of a lonely, isolated person unable to reach out and touch anyone beyond the bars of his cage, but really it is one of the most public acts anyone can commit. It immediately transfers ownership of the suicide's life to the body public. Even if you go to your grave with your secrets "intact," it opens your every deed and thought to speculation and interpretation by complete strangers at a level unknown even to the most extroverted public figure. The kind of salacious gossip and public psychoanalysis to which celebrities who flame out very publicly are subject is nothing compared with the commentary surrounding a suicide. You always own at least a part of your life—legally, emotionally, intellectually, spiritually—while you are alive; you give all that up when you kill yourself. Everybody owns a suicide, which is why the victim's friends and families find themselves in the untenable guardianship of public property. It is as if you committed suicide at the beginning of your life rather than at the end of it, so that nothing you ever did is allowed to be seen outside of that context.

For his last album, released posthumously, Smith wrote a song called "King's Crossing," in which he seems to excoriate himself for having mined his emotional life for public consumption. "The method acting that pays my bills / Keeps a fat man feeding in Beverly Hills . . . I get my check from the trash treasury / Because I took my own insides out." It is also the song that is most often quoted by pundits who believe that his entire body of work was a paean and prelude to suicide. "I can't prepare for death any more than I already have," he sings, and it is easy to believe him. He seems to be making the link between suicide and selling out pretty unequivocally. His friend E. V. Day spelled it out explicitly: "He didn't like himself. He was turning into a person that he would hate . . . I think he sort of lost the ability to fight to be the individual that he wanted to be."

A lot of people fantasize about what it would be like to be famous and to have somebody else's life and talent. We think, How great would it be to have a talent like Bob Dylan's or John Updike's, to have the glamorous life of a movie star? I think it's fair to say that few of us, no matter how sincerely we might wish to have a musical gift like Elliott Smith's, would want to be him or to have his life. Yes, we might casually entertain the fantasy of entering into some Faustian bargain, trading happiness for divine inspiration, but that's only because we know it will never happen. A few years ago, I translated a nonfiction book called *Happiness*, by Matthieu Ricard, a Frenchman who in his youth gave up a brilliant career in molecular genetics to become a Buddhist monk in Nepal. In the book, Ricard talks about his amazement at how many people resist the notion of happiness, or of striving for happiness, because they equate it with giving up an important component of their individuality. Like Tolstoy, who opens *Anna Karenina* with the infamous assertion that all happy families are alike while each unhappy family is unhappy in its own way, they believe that there is something bland, generic, and unambitious about being content with your lot. Happy people are all the same because, having no cause to assess the failures of their life or their own part in them, they lack introspection; unhappy people are all unique, and deep. But as Ricard and Socrates both know, nobody actually wants to be unhappy, even if they imagine they do. They simply convince themselves that it's easier and safer to cling to that leaky boat and spend their life bailing than it is to strike out and swim for solid ground, when in fact it is neither.

I couldn't say whether Elliott Smith was one of those people. He claimed to have been abused by his stepfather as a child, but he was educated enough to know that there are many different avenues for healing childhood traumas, and he never took any of them. In fact, he became angry and indignant at any friend who tried to help him, or help him help himself, and even broke off old friendships and professional relationships on that account. Most of us, I think, have perfectly plausible rationales for not seeking the help we need, if we need any, or doing the things we need to do to become happier, and Smith seems in that sense to have been no different from anybody else. But where we may want to see him as apart from the rest of us is that he had a gift—an incredible, unique gift—and when someone with a gift fails to make the best possible use of it, we feel that he has somehow let the rest of us down—those of us who wish we had a gift like his and imagine that, if it were ours, we would not fail to be grateful and to make the best possible use of it.

Goethe said: "The person born with a talent they are meant to use will find their greatest happiness in using it," but that is demonstrably untrue, as the stories of Smith and countless others like him attest. How, we ask ourselves, could someone write such beautiful music and yet not derive enough satisfaction from his own genius—in the classical sense, the tutelary deity, the generative force of the creative impulse—to save his own life? Where is the sense of arrival, of triumph, of destiny well met, that we expect from an artist who, like Henry Moore, is both comprehensively fulfilled by his life's work and recognized for it. Didn't he know how lucky he was? If I could fashion such a beautiful, transcendent thing, we tell ourselves, I'd make the most of it; I would never squander the opportunities it afforded me. If I had Elliott Smith's gift, it would make me happy, not sad. If I had Elliott Smith's life, or Kurt Cobain's life, or David Foster Wallace's life, he would still be alive. He'd be fulfilled.

But that, patently, is not so. For one thing, while Smith's gift may not have been enough to save his life—as if a great talent for something were some kind of talisman or air bag that gives its possessor improved protection against life's vicissitudes or his own foibles—it most certainly wasn't what killed him. What killed him was his inability to find sufficient reason to stay alive, and that was entirely independent of his ability to create great art. You can absolutely make the best use of your talent, as Smith did by writing so many lovely, shattering songs, and still have a miserable life. And of course, there are plenty of people who would argue that Elliott Smith could never have done what he did if he had been happy and well-adjusted. So when we talk about the artist's need to create, and the sense of fulfillment that creating art must provide over and above monetary or status considerations, it becomes obvious that this need and its satisfaction have nothing to do with happiness. The hunger artist doesn't make herself *happy* by engaging her genius—she simply fuels her hunger. It is not about pleasure at all; it is about survival. As Smith said, "You're so lonely in this individuality that in a way there is no payoff. You're just trying to do more of what you do and stay alive."

Again and again, we find flaws in Henry Moore's argument that the secret of life is to find fulfillment in the work you were born to do. Moore characterized this work as a "task"—in other words, your work is the process, not its outcome. You are fulfilled not by producing a certain number of sculptures, or songs, or novels, or widgets, or spicy tuna hand rolls, but by the impossible labor of producing just one perfect sample thereof. That is what we are taught and what most of us believe, or want to believe, because it comforts our sense of being a unique individual with a singular talent and destiny. Which is precisely why someone like Henry Moore can get away with intoning oracular falsehoods. Our experience tells us otherwise; our experience tells us that doing our life's work—whether it is making art, raising children, running a business, advancing scholarship, or simply healing an ancient wound—is not always going to meet our expectations of fulfillment; it may, instead, simply be our way of treading water, of staying alive. Yet instead of trying a different tack—instead of telling Henry Moore to go fuck himself and heading off to find our own ways of being happy—we assume that we are just going about it the wrong way, and commit ourselves even deeper to the failed path.

For so long, I made myself miserable because I believed that the necessity of holding down a full-time job was keeping me from the one task I was born to do and that could fulfill me. I knew, or thought I knew, that I could be happy if only I had the opportunity to devote myself to that task, as Moore, Rilke, Goethe, Yeats, and every right-thinking philosopher, artist, and sociologist had prescribed since time immemorial. I wrote book after book, each one a little better than the last, yet despite all the abundant evidence I remained convinced that this work was not fulfilling—that I was not a happy person—because I was doing it wrong, I wasn't giving it my all, I hadn't sacrificed enough to it.

But I wasn't doing it wrong; like Elliott Smith, I was doing it right, creating the best work I was capable of creating, but

I was blaming it for failing to reciprocate with a reward that it was not capable of bestowing. My work was there to keep me alive, and it was doing exactly what it was supposed to do, but I was asking it to make me happy, and that was not its job. Finding a way to somehow live my "real" life was no solution because I was already living my real life. And making more room in my life to allow my work to perform a task it was never designed to perform was not going to help; it was only going to increase my frustration and make things worse. You can kennel your dog in a glittering ballroom and it still won't dance the waltz; nor is your gift, your work, a treasure that must be put to positive use in order to make the world a better and safer place. It was never in the cards for me to be a better writer, or a happier person, by living the life I thought Geoff Dyer had stolen from me, and I'm convinced that the same holds true for anyone who believes that more freedom to do what they love would make them happier. Elliott Smith had all the freedom in the world to do what he loved, and he was a poor, hapless bastard—nobody's victim, for sure. It's being happier that makes you happy, not doing something else, or more of the same thing. You can say this in all conviction, of course, and still be unable to make it happen. That, I suppose, is something we each need to figure out for ourselves.

No one could look at Franz Kafka and call him a happy person, either. Most of the major patterns that governed his life, work, and thoughts are well enough known in outline: he continued to live with his parents for most of his life, despite complaining about them incessantly and having a deeply fraught relationship with his father; he remained in the same job—the state workers' insurance bureaucracy—for almost his entire professional life, and complained bitterly about that, too; he was wrenchingly ambivalent about romantic commitment, and as a result repeatedly failed in his entanglements despite a yearning for emotional stability; he wrote obsessively, yet never made any great effort to complete what he wrote, and published very little in his lifetime; he was sexually voracious, yet oddly repelled by physical intimacy. Another thing that was certainly true about Franz Kafka, as he himself insisted, was that it was writing that kept him alive. Oddly enough, it was as he lay starving to death, unable to eat because of his advanced laryngeal tuberculosis, that he put the finishing touches to "A Hunger Artist."

After a miserable childhood of being emotionally bullied and browbeaten by his vulgarian father, and a youth crushed and asphyxiated by an educational system of merciless stupefaction, and almost immediately upon completing the legal studies that he had desperately sought to avoid, Franz Kafka took the post in the state bureaucracy that he was to hold and to loathe until his dying day. This is the capsule biography of the Kafka who, when they think about him at all, most people seem to recognize—a man entrapped by his own neuroses, an artist forced by the demands of the real world to squander his gifts and, in the phrasing of one biographer, to suffer the "martyrdom" of "killing time." Although he generally recognized that his quandary was more complex and multifaceted than that, Kafka essentially subscribed to this view himself. Although he had spent his entire adult life unhappily fulfilling what he saw to be his duties, he did not accept that he had yet begun to live his real life, blaming even his preternaturally youthful looks on this paralysis. "I need only throw my work in the office out of this complex," he wrote in his diary, "in order to begin my real life in which, with the progress of my work, my face will finally be able to age in a natural way." Kafka's job at the Worker's Accident Insurance Institute lasted from 1908, less than a year after he had completed his obligatory unpaid clerical apprenticeship, until his death in 1924, so it is fair to say that this predicament was the focal, and focusing, obsession of his entire professional life. In a nutshell, as he put it, "That I, so long as I am not freed of my office, am simply lost, that is clearer to me than anything else, it is just a matter, as long as it is possible, of holding my head so high that I do not drown."

Kafka's bitter complaints about the demands and constraints his job placed on his writing life are exhaustively documented. They are all variants of the statement "Above all else, it is clear to me that I am simply lost until I can break free of the office," and they are all, of course, eloquent and heartfelt. But there is a repetitious quality about them that inclines me to share them very sparingly here. And that is doubly true because they were often expressed ambivalently, and also because they tell only one side of the story.

Although Kafka's biographer Ernst Pawel was surely correct in asserting that "writing . . . was his sole reason for living, and his sole means of keeping alive," Kafka was not unaware of the advantages of holding a secure, reasonably well-paid job with the state. For one thing, he continually referred to his precarious health as one reason why he could not contemplate a life as a freelance writer. It's not entirely clear to me what he meant by this. Because his superiors were remarkably generous to him with paid leaves of absence to attend to his various ailments real and psychosomatic, it's possible that he believed that as a freelance or professional writer he couldn't afford to lose income when he was ill. Presumably, too, he enjoyed particularly generous health benefits as a state employee. But it's more likely that what he was referring to was the anxiety and stress that accompany the freelance life, where no job is too small to accept and your income is only as reliable as your last paycheck. It is undoubtedly true that the inconvenience of having to schedule your writing life around your professional life is at least partly mitigated by the fact that you don't wake up in the middle of the night worrying about money, which can be equally or even more enervating than having to clock in every day. If that was the case with Kafka—if he understood enough about himself to know that he would find the freelance life and its relentless stressors more debilitating than holding down a demanding but secure position—then at least some of his complaining was insincere, or at least conveniently forgetful. But then, of course, we all sometimes forget the truths that clash inconveniently with the myths with which we man the ramparts of our egos, and there's no reason why Kafka should be held more strictly to account on that score than we hold ourselves.

Kafka was also very careful to keep his professional and creative lives separate and distinct. As his close friend, literary executor, and biographer Max Brod pointed out, "When it came to the point of having to make a living, Franz insisted that the job have nothing to do with literature; that would have seemed to him a debasement of literary creativity." Kafka may have been afraid that, if he had to make a living by his pen, he would be compelled to take on assignments on the basis not of their literary merits but of their ability to help him pay the bills; knowing what we do about him, there can be no doubt that being a hack, even if only in his own mind, would have been the source of even more anguish than being a salaried civil servant with office hours.

There were other ways, too, in which Kafka intuitively understood what was good for himself without necessarily acknowledging it. As Pawel points out, Kafka's post in the upper management of the state bureaucracy carried with it a kind of prestige that, while he may have been reluctant to admit it, was not without meaning to the son of a tradesman—a grown man who continued to live with his parents well into his thirties, and a Jew, of whom there were virtually none at his level. For Kafka was hardly a Dickensian clerk hunched over his desk copying accounts by candlelight—he was a high-ranking official with important responsibilities for the welfare of hundreds of thousands of workers. The work gave his life "a structure and status on which he came to depend for a large measure of identity and self-respect," while the lavish approval of his superiors, with whom he got along very well—"Combines outstanding zeal with sustained interest in all assignments" . . . "Dr. Kafka is an eminently hardworking employee endowed with exceptional talent and devotion to duty" . . . "Without Kafka, the whole department would collapse"—could not be easily dismissed by someone who otherwise received little recognition for his creativity. Let's remember that Kafka published very little in his lifetime and that, although his work was known and admired by a small circle of German-speaking intellectuals in Prague, he had little opportunity outside his office to receive and enjoy such unreserved praise. And none of us—not even Franz Kafka, who was his own bitterest critic—is entirely immune to praise, no matter what the source. The fact is, a person rarely does as well at his job as Kafka did without enjoying it at some level. In that light, all his bitter complaining has to be seen at least in part as a way of occulting the satisfactions of his professional life that, as a literary man to the bone, he could not quite bring himself to acknowledge. To Kafka, the only life that mattered was the writing life, and the only work that mattered was literature; it would have been painful and disorienting for him to admit any other realm of experience—but most especially his hated job—as a source of pleasure or generator of self-confidence.

Finally, there were so many other hurdles, self-imposed and otherwise, between Kafka and any belief in the possibility of living a fulfilled life that his professional obligations begin to seem the very least among them. As Pawel says, "the obstacles in his path had very little to do with outward circumstances." They were the very same obstacles that prevented him from breaking with his father and setting up his own home, from committing himself to marriage, and from ever completing and publishing an extended work of fiction to his own satisfaction. His job offered him a pretext to complain about emotional handicaps that he was very well aware of but apparently powerless to overcome. In the same way, he received his diagnosis of tuberculosis not as the death sentence it was, but as a blessing and a liberation—at last he could point to something even more concrete and explicit than his job that released him from all responsibility for his condition. As Max Brod said, "Kafka sees [his TB] as psychogenic, his salvation from marriage, so to speak. He calls it his final defeat. But has been sleeping well ever since. Liberated? Tormented soul."

The harpy that most tormented Kafka's soul was doubt, which I think is why, in the century of relativity, not only his work but his entire life spoke so immediately to us. Almost a hundred years after his death, we continue to read him, literally and figuratively, as a contemporary. "My condition is not unhappiness, but it is also not happiness, not indifference, not weakness, not fatigue, not another interest—so what is it then?" That is the very voice of the twentieth century speaking. Every aspect, every dark corner, every shining surface of his life and work is examined in the light of doubt, slashed asunder by the blade of doubt, restitched by the needle of doubt, and resurrected by the faith of doubt. "My doubts stand in a circle around every word, I see them before I see the word, but what then! I do not see the word at all, I invent it." Doubt was the very medium in which his every thought, every action, every sexual neurosis, and every literary impulse was cultured and nourished. Doubting—about his literary capacities, about his ability to love, about the possibility of marriage and a shared life, about his Jewish identity and its meaning, about his place in the world of German letters, about his own lovability, about the possibility of happiness—was not Kafka's handicap. It was his identity and his worldview, his oxygen and his religion, and there is no way to envision a Kafka who had freed himself from those doubts—a Kafka, say, who had successfully quit his job, emancipated himself from his hang-ups about his father, and escaped the smothering embrace of Prague, his "little mother with claws"—remaining Kafka as we know him. "That which is possible will surely happen," he wrote in his dairy. "Only that which happens is possible." The only possible Kafka was the Kafka who happened. "This morning, for the first time in a long time, the joy again of imagining a knife twisted in my heart." With the exception of Elliott Smith, there is no one else on earth who could plausibly have written that.

I find it very painful to read Kafka's complaints about the demands of his job, partly because they sound so much like my own, but also because, unlike him, I have voices of reason whispering in my ear, pointing out where I repeat myself over and over, where I have the power to make changes, where I have options. So I can both empathize fully with Kafka's sense of powerlessness, and also see where he could have helped himself and did not. It is true that he was subject to certain social constraints and proprieties that I am not, but for someone who claimed to be so unhappy and so vexed by his predicament, these would hardly have been insurmountable. Indeed, by the time of his death he had largely begun to overcome them, and there is some reason to believe that, had he not died so young, he would have succeeded entirely in breaking away from his family, his job, and his nightmares of bondage. In his last lover, Dora Diamant, he had found someone who was not inhibited by social proprieties or by fears of penury, and he might very well have learned to live by her example. It is far from inconceivable that they may have been married, had children, emigrated to Palestine.

The one thing we do know is that things could not have been other than they were for the many poor, unhappy geniuses who have been unable to find any quiet despite their gifts. We all know that money can't buy you love or happiness, but I think that anyone who has ever heard the life stories of Kafka, or Vincent van Gogh, or Robert Johnson, has had a moment when he has wished that he could travel back in time and make their lives a little easier, among other things by somehow giving them the financial independence they always claimed to desire (but also, perhaps, by demonstrating their clairvoyance and artistic vision by being the first to recognize the artist's genius). This isn't an unreasonable fantasy. After all, Rainer Maria Rilke spent much of his poetic career living off other people's largesse; what if Kafka had had similar moxie? Flaubert came into a sizable inheritance in his midtwenties that changed the course of his life and gave him the leisure to hone his perfectionism; what if something similar had happened to Van Gogh?

So my impulse is to want to travel back in time and search Kafka out in one of the literary cafés he liked to haunt, and sit down and have a good chat with him. Since this is a fantasy, we will both have to be able to speak a language that one of us doesn't actually know, so I will generously assume that burden and learn German before I leave. I will also need to prepare in advance a way to convince him that I am really from the future. The easiest way to do that, of course, would be to bring him copies of books that he had not yet written, perhaps in multiple languages, but that would be fraught with all sorts of causality paradoxes of the kind found in science fiction. What if, for instance, I were to bring him a copy of *The Castle* just as he was beginning to work on a novel about a naughty little kitten, which he would then abandon in favor of *The Castle*? I would have been responsible for depriving the world of the Kafka novel about the kitten, and I'm not sure how I would live with that. But to avoid being distracted, let's say that I was able to travel back in time, that I chose to use this amazing power to have a heart-to-heart talk with Franz Kafka, that I learned German for the occasion, and that I was able to persuade him of the authenticity and sincerity of my mission. What would I say to him?

I suppose I would begin by introducing myself. I am an American novelist of the late twentieth and early twenty-first centuries, I would say, and like him a Jew of Eastern European origin. At the time of this writing, I am already ten years older than he was at his death, but it might be indiscreet to mention the fact that I know precisely the date, place, and circumstances of his death. Instead, I would focus on what he and I have in common. Like you, I would tell him, I am the author of a handful of novels and other works. I know beyond a doubt that your books are immeasurably better than mine will ever be, and I can live with that, but I also know (because

I've read all your letters and diaries—sorry about that) that you and I entertain very similar doubts about our respective talents and that we both often despair about the possibility of expressing ourselves adequately. I assure you that the world has already pronounced itself and found yours to be one of the towering, enduring voices of world literature. A generation after your death, you will be famous around the globe, translated into dozens if not hundreds of languages, so you can now lay to rest any worries you may have entertained about whether your labors were worth it. I know you weren't writing for fame and glory, but even once you're dead it can't hurt to know that the people of my time still value your work at the very highest level. That's a big advantage you have over me, but let's not go there just now. Instead, let's focus on what is making you so unhappy.

I know that one central dilemma of your existence is the need to support yourself while always striving to preserve the quiet, stress-free space that will allow your inner voice to rise and be heard. This is how you put it in your diary in 1911:

Aside from my family relationships, I could not live by literature if only, to begin with, because of the slow maturing of my work and its special character; besides, I am prevented also by my health and my character from devoting myself to what is, in the most favourable case, an uncertain life. I have therefore become an official in a social insurance agency. Now these two professions can never be reconciled with one another and admit a common fortune. The smallest good fortune in one becomes a great misfortune in the other. If I have written something good one evening, I am afire the next day in the office and can bring nothing to completion. This back and forth continually becomes worse. Outwardly, I fulfill my duties satisfactorily in the office, not my inner duties, however, and every unfulfilled inner duty becomes a misfortune that never leaves.

If you swapped "a social insurance agency" for "the international civil service," this could be an entry in my diary, if I kept one. So I completely understand your feeling of being trapped, of being "unresistingly fixed wherever I happen to be," as you wrote elsewhere. You cannot live in a world that forces such compromises upon you, yet you feel utterly powerless to alter your circumstances. That, too, I understand, although the world is rightly unforgiving in its scorn for educated, middle-class white men who feel helpless to make changes, because if people like us are not able to do it, who is? So we have to be careful not only how we couch our quandary before our peers, but also how we frame our problem even to ourselves, in the privacy of our despair—for if we continue to define ourselves as victims of our own indecision we become the forges and smithies of the very chains that hold us down. The world has forgiven you this weakness, Franz, because of the use you made of it, at the price of your own misery, but the rest of us may not be so lucky. We need to take a long, honest look at ourselves and figure out how to draw sustenance from our experience, and to see ourselves as the authors of our own destinies, because the world will not forgive us if we don't, and we will definitely never be the artists, or the parents, or the friends, or the decent, loving, open human beings we hope to become.

Let's take a look at this life in which you are entrapped like a fly on flypaper. First of all, let us remember that all people, unless they are independently wealthy, have somehow to make a living, and that the wealthy are no happier than we are. Although we convince ourselves that we would know how to be happy and grateful and productive if we had their advantages, there is no empirical proof and very little precedent to support that argument. So, as writers we are faced with a stark, simple choice: either we set out to make our living by our pen, by writing what we know will sell enough to feed, clothe, and house us and our families, or we write precisely what suits us and we stop complaining about how we have to find an alternate income. Some writers are not faced with that problem—no one would accuse Stephen King or Philip Roth of prostituting their talents to make a buck—but you are not one of those, Franz, as you know very well, and by all evidence neither am I, much as I'd like to be. And by the way, the same rule applies to everyone, not just writers—we all need to find something to do that someone is willing to pay us to do.

So, Franz, you have a job. Welcome to the world. Yes, I know that you are a little more high-strung than the rest of us; we can and do make certain allowances for that, but after all you survived twelve brutal years of schooling and the even more soul-crushing years of law school, so perhaps you are not as fragile as you think you are. I would also remind you that you quit your first job after only a few months because it did not give you enough time to write, and that you took your present position precisely because your work day ends at 2:00 p.m., giving you enough leisure and income not only to write but also to go to the theater, travel, loiter in cafés with your fellow litterateurs, and go whoring to your heart's content. So no matter how powerless it may suit you to see yourself, you have a demonstrated ability to take big decisions to improve your circumstances. In fact, there is not one aspect of your circumstances that is not the result of a deliberate choice you have made. Being chained to a desk job, living with your mother and father well into your thirties, your failure to find a wife, your aloneness, even your relative obscurity as a writer during your own lifetime—all the result of being not a passive object of fate but an active protagonist and prime mover in your own story. There is nothing powerless about you at all other than your inability to visualize yourself as anything but powerless. When you kick against the pricks and strain against the traces, it is not a charade, exactly, or a pretense, but it is an act of aggression against yourself.

And let's also acknowledge that, in your lighter moments, you are able to recognize that it's not all or always that bad. You hate to admit it, because it is a vulgar and philistine weakness that belongs to the likes of your father, but you enjoy the little perks that come with a regular income and a respectable position in life—what you call your "more than ordinary inclination toward a comfortable life." The nice clothes, the vacations, the theater, the café life, the respect of powerful men and the gratitude of your downtrodden clients, the plummy associations with the elite, high-brow Germanic culture of Bohemia and its cultured Jews, rather than with the earthy, passionate Czech proletariat and the semiliterate Jews of the East—these are advantages that distinguish you from your loud, aggressive, mercenary father, who grew up pushing a wheelbarrow, and that give you secret gratification as his creature. As you write in your diary,

> *I caught myself thinking . . . that I could put up with my present situation very contentedly, and that I only had to be careful not to have all my time free for literature. I had scarcely exposed this thought to a closer inspection when it became no longer astonishing and already appeared accustomed. I disputed my ability to devote all my time to literature.*

The truth is, if you devoted all your time to business—not only your insurance job, but also the asbestos factory in which you are a minor partner with your brother-in-law—you would feel too much like your father, but if you devoted all your time to writing, as you generally claim to wish to do, you'd probably have to give up most of the little pleasures and comforts that make your overwrought life halfway bearable. And even you, Franz, can't write fourteen hours a day.

Then there's the issue of family. You complain bitterly about your "inability to endure life alone," and claim your bachelorhood to be the calvary you are prepared to endure for your art. "Alone, I could perhaps some day really give up my job. Married, it will never be possible." In other words, you remain a lonely bachelor in order to preserve the possibility that you can one day quit your job and write full-time. That, at least, is what you tell your married friends, and although they may well envy your lack of responsibilities, they may also wonder why you don't actually make use of your freedom to do what you are always claiming you want to do—

quit your job or, at the very least, move out of your parents' apartment, where the very thought of your mother and father in bed together—provoked by something as innocuous as their bedroom door slightly ajar—is enough to make you dizzy with nausea.

And yet, in almost the very same breath, you make a totally contradictory argument.

I must be alone a great deal. What I accomplished was only the result of being alone . . . The fear of the connexion, of passing into the other. Then I'll never be alone again . . .

One minute you are incapable of being alone, the next you are in mortal terror of having to share your life. I wonder if you are even fully aware that you carry these two conflicting worldviews within yourself, and that because you are too afraid to let one go you must always juggle them, one always firmly in hand while the other is momentarily out of sight overhead.

There is nothing wrong with being ambivalent, especially about something that you genuinely cannot change. But what you seem to imagine to be a condition peculiar to your unique, tortured weltanschauung is in fact a perfectly standard appurtenance of modern middle-class existence, hardly limited to neurotic, angst-ridden Middle European writers romantically doomed to an intense, lonely inner life and early death (sorry!). In fact, though I hate to say it, it is probably at least in part because you are able in your work to so convincingly create a universe structured on and glued together by your own ambivalence, doubt, and powerlessness that the people of the modern world have responded to it in such a universal and personal way. We all know what it's like to feel powerless, and hopefully we can be empathetic without being enablers. Just because you are not, in fact, powerless doesn't necessarily make it any easier. I get it; I think many of us get it; we feel for you, just as we hope that people will not judge us too harshly for feeling less in control than we really are, for all sorts of psychological reasons stretching back into a murky childhood. You are not alone in this, Franz, and you needn't feel alone—I can help you to get a firmer grasp on the issues that are holding you back, and show you that they are all of your own making. You can be happier, if that is what you want. You can have the girl—Felice, Milena, or Dora, your pick—and she will be a help and a companion to you, rather than a drain on your energies; you can have the job, even if it isn't always a joy, and the comforts that come with it, which you know you appreciate; you can live away from your father and break the debilitating addiction to your resentment; you can even have children, and do your work late at night, or early in the morning, or in the library, as I do. You may even find that they provide you with inspiration—or, god forbid, with hope.

If I were to wander into Prague's Café Arco one blustery winter's evening in the first decade of the twentieth century, and find Franz Kafka deep in animated conversation there among his circle of friends, this is the general outline of what I might be tempted to tell him. You don't have to be sad; just keep doing what you're doing and see it for the gift it is. Keep doubting, but act despite your doubt. Publish your beautiful books during your own lifetime, marry the woman you love, raise your children in harmony, gentleness, and tolerance, escape the stranglehold of tradition and fear. You, too, can be happy if you allow yourself to be.

It hardly bears pointing out that this is all the biggest crock—and not only because, if I had the ability to time-travel, I'm not convinced that I would use it to attempt the quixotic mission of turning Franz Kafka into a well-balanced, cheerful optimist. For one thing, Kafka had a coterie of devoted friends, Max Brod chief among them, who were engaged, productive, empowered, and intellectual professionals—if they were unable to help him see the many ways in which he worked to undermine himself and his own work, it is unlikely that I could. I'm pretty sure that it would be a thankless task, just as it was for the many friends of Elliott Smith who sought to help him. And of course it would not just be Kafka himself who would fail to thank me or to go on to live a happier life thanks to my intervention. It's hard to imagine how I would manage to escape universal opprobrium for what would surely be perceived as a misguided attempt to deprive the twentieth century of one of its most important, vibrant, and idiosyncratic voices. Because how could anybody imagine *The Trial* or "The Metamorphosis" or "The Judgment"—the composition of which Kafka described as "a true birth, covered with filth and slime"—having been written by a content, serene middle-aged civil servant who had reconciled himself to the world's cruel absurdities, was confident in his own talents and the public's interest in his work, and was capable of accepting and giving love in all good faith and trust? I know I couldn't, and that being the case, why would it be in anybody's interest to deprive the world of such eternal artistry for the sake of the happiness of one ephemeral individual—especially one who was destined to die at forty-one no matter how cheerful and emotionally fulfilled I had made him?

Since I am not Franz Kafka or Elliott Smith, and I am not ever likely to produce work at their level, does that mean that I should feel free to work on being happier than I am, since I will not be depriving the world of great works but I will be making my life, and the lives of those who know and love me, tangibly more satisfying and rewarding? Somehow, when put like that, it sounds petty, callow, and vain, yet it is, in broad strokes, the problem that, in varied but analogous forms, most of us have to contend with at some point in our lives. How much can we give of our selves before we start giving ourselves away? How much of our selves can we keep for ourselves before we have nothing left to give? Those are the questions that hunger artists are forced by the nature of their commitments and their devotions to ask themselves every day. By all evidence, they are no closer to answering them than the rest of us are. The problem is that the obvious answer—"just enough"—is going to satisfy no one at all. "Just enough" is no one's recipe for a life lived to its full potential.

But of course you don't have to be a hunger artist, or an artist of any sort, to feel the full relevance of those questions to your life. Kafka knew all about the road not taken. It was the one in which he had remained unmarried and was able to quit his job: "Bachelor. I remain pure. I focus all my strength. Responsible only for myself. No worries, concentrating on work." But everyone has his or her unlived life, perhaps more than one, that is every bit as vibrant and aspirational and only just as barely out of reach as Kafka's. The parent—and very especially the mother—entertains the unlived life where she can do it all, or where she hasn't given up her career to raise children, or where she has been able to give up her career to raise her children, or where she has had no children and devotes herself wholeheartedly to something or someone else. The corporate man who, in his unlived life, owns a small business and answers to no one, or has risen to the top and is able to run things his way, or has dropped out of the rat race altogether and raises goats on a mountainside. The school principal who, in her unlived life, has passed up the opportunity for advancement and stuck with the hands-on teaching that was her first love. The married man who, on the road not taken, has treated his wife with all the love and respect she deserves, or has left a loveless marriage that ought to have been dismantled long before, or has always stayed with his high school sweetheart and never known another love.

My thoughts return here to Adam Phillips and his contention that "in our unlived lives, we are always more satisfied, far less frustrated versions of ourselves." That may be true, yet your unlived life is not necessarily far-fetched. It may be a fantasy only in the sense that it is the one you did not choose.

It is not necessarily Paul Gauguin abandoning his wife and children to paint and fuck teenage girls in Tahiti; it is merely the suit you chose not to buy in favor of the suit you actually bought. It's walking to work up Madison Avenue instead of Fifth. It's ordering risotto instead of the sea bream. That being the case, the question arises: If you were living that alternate life, what would your fantasy life be? Do you imagine for one second that your wants would be fewer, that you would somehow be satisfied? Phillips claims that "we want only what isn't there," but that is not at all true. Far more often, we want what we already have but fail to recognize it as the thing we want. The difference between our lived lives and our unlived lives may only be one of perspective.

It is because of that understanding, and not despite it, that these unlived lives are not only healthy but essential to our mental health as the best available and most viable aspirational models for us to follow. We do not necessarily need to attain them, or even believe we can attain them, because, as Phillips rightly notes, "satisfaction is no more the solution to frustration than certainty is the solution to skepticism." In other words, we may have to teach ourselves to live with the idea that it is probably in nourishing the frustrations of our unlived lives, rather than in satisfying them—in cherishing and protecting our inner hunger artist, rather than in letting him loose upon the world—that we come closest to being the person we most fully wish to be and to living the lives we most fully wish to live. I think this may be the vision that Elliott Smith was groping for when he wrote about "fight[ing] problems with bigger problems," but oddly enough, for all his emotional blind spots and blinding despair, it was Kafka who put his finger on it:

> *Anyone who cannot come to terms with his life while he is alive needs one hand to ward off a little his despair over his fate—he has little success in this—but with his other hand he can note down what he sees among the ruins, for he sees different (and more) things than do the others.*

The Therapist

In *Dying and Creating: A Search for Meaning*, Rosemary Gordon's minor classic of analytical psychology, the author posits four stages in the creative process. The first is the preparatory stage, "when a person immerses himself in a problem and feels himself drawn into a period of conscious concern and struggle." Next comes the incubation stages, when "a person 'sleeps on the problem' either literally or metaphorically." The third stage is that of illumination. "There is, as it were, a sudden flash of light, a sudden catching of one's breath. An idea has 'occurred' to him." The last is the stage of verification, "a period of critical testing, when the ideas received in the period of inspiration are tested."

Gordon is very careful to point out that "creative" does not always mean "artistic," in as much as the creative process she outlines may be the same whether it is engaged in by a poet, a painter, a scientist, an engineer, an inventor, or, most emphatically, a psychoanalyst. Even so, she concedes that because making art involves "a particularly large number of different mental activities . . . much of the little we know about the nature of the creative process we owe to the self-examination and introspective work of artists."

I can't speak for any other writer, but I would have to say that the stages defined by Gordon do roughly coincide with my personal experience of writing novels. The preparation would be the ill-defined stage when the idea for a book first begins to take form in my psyche. That form may manifest itself first as the outline of a character, a vague or crystal-clear idea for a story, a dream, a sentence or sentence fragment that becomes locked on auto-replay in my mind, a location or even nothing more than a feeling. The concept for my first novel came to me fully formed in a matter of moments as I stood before a statue in the old Museum of Modern Art in Paris; that for my second as I sat in traffic on a crosstown bus in Manhattan, observing the lunchtime crowds in Bryant Park; yet for my next I am stuck with nothing more than an image of a young girl conversing with a group of teenage ghosts in a beach house in Southeast Asia. All of these fall neatly into Gordon's concept of preparation.

Gordon presents such inchoate images as "problems," and she's right—the writer immediately recognizes that his task is to appropriate this infinitesimal nugget of information or emotion and unwrap it, resolve it as a mathematician resolves an equation, to perfect internal coherence. If it does not present itself as a problem to be solved, or at the very least as a challenge to be met headlong, it is probably not the right project for the artist to adopt at that moment and should be set aside, though not necessarily discarded, as it may ripen to maturity at a later date.

Incubation is the time between the first recognition of an idea for a project and its execution. Again, I have no idea how this works with other artists. A poet or a songwriter may experience no perceptible lapse of time at all between preparation and illumination—that is, he or she may receive an idea for a poem or a song and sit down immediately to work on it. That doesn't necessarily mean that the incubation stage did not occur; it may simply be that an experienced poet, keenly in tune with her own creative process, recognizes the precise moment that a poem is ready to be born and runs it through an incubation stage accelerated to the speed of thought, or else that incubation and illumination—that is, the deliberate nurturing of the seed and its fruition on paper—are melded into a single stage. In my case, however, incubation can take a very long time. I generally spend more time thinking about a book than I do actually writing it down. This seems normal to me, the mature outcome of decades of patient practice, and it makes me wonder whether it is at the root of why so many people are able to distinguish between so-called literary writing and genre writing, in which the incubation period is necessarily curtailed by the imperatives of the production line.

As for the stage of inspiration or illumination, I take this as referring to the task of producing a work of art or any other product of the creative process. It certainly does not manifest as an aha moment for an artist, scientist, or engineer, who may spend years immersed in this phase of her work, but it still holds true that it can be represented as an acknowledgment that a mental threshold has been crossed allowing "physical" work to begin on the project. Also, of course, within the protracted process, there will be many moments of inspiration that strike the creator as a sudden blossoming of an immature idea.

It's pretty obvious what Gordon's verification means to, say, a scientist or an economist. For a writer, I suppose it corresponds to the editing process, or the time when the artist assesses the validity of her work either by sharing it with close, trusted friends or colleagues, or simply by reading, singing, or playing it through to determine its adequacy. So far in my career, I have twice discarded completed first drafts because the book they were trying to be was unsalvageable. It hasn't been pleasant, for sure, but it has been necessary. This is of course a much more common course of action for painters, songwriters, and poets, who presumably can afford to be more spontaneous about their work than I can, because it takes them hours or days, rather than years, to complete.

I don't want to attach more importance to Gordon's definition of the creative process than she does herself. It is only a small part of her book, which is focused on the connection between the ability to recognize and overcome one's fear of death (through analysis) and the ability to unleash one's creative impulses. "Those who would die well and those would create well are people who must be capable of being open and available both to the life forces and the death forces." She is not being esoteric here in her reference to "forces." By "life forces" she means differentiation of the ego, and by "death forces" she means reintegration of the self into the undifferentiated universe, thereby opening a window onto a vast landscape of Jungian analytical psychology about which I am supremely unqualified to write. No, what interests me far more in Gordon's definition of the creative process is the fact that, inadvertently or no, it would seem to apply not just to the production of a single piece of work, but with equal or greater accuracy to the entire arc of the creative life, from birth to maturity. In fact, its four stages jibe, with an amazing amount of overlap, with the first four phases of adult life that I've identified in my subtitle and chapter headings. "Preparation" matches up with "ambition," "incubation" with "love," "illumination" with "freedom" and "verification" with "fulfillment." In both Gordon's and my timeline, "wisdom" is what comes with and following upon an enlightened understanding of all that has gone before.

At the most basic level of meaning (which is the only level at which I'm able to address it), Jungian psychology starts out on the premise that a child is born with a sense of wholeness, or integration, with the world around it, which Jung calls the "self." Gradually, however, it develops an ego-consciousness whereby it differentiates itself from the world and from other people. The process of successful differentiation is the ego's principal task for the first half of one's life. Once that has been achieved, Jung believed, the remainder of a healthy life, in which the individual has developed a clear and secure sense of who he is in relation to himself and others, will be devoted to individuation, that is, the deliberate rediscovery of the self and a desire to restore the sense of wholeness with which he was born. Clearly, within that scheme, Gordon's first two phases of the creative process, preparation and incubation, can stand in for childhood and young adulthood— ego differentiation—while the third and fourth, illumination and verification, correspond to mature adulthood and the task of individuation. Even admitting that I may have gotten some of this wrong—after all, everything I know about analytical psychology is set down on the previous few pages—the phases of adulthood that I've tried to define and illustrate in this book are an eerie echo of Gordon's schedule. Preparation, incubation, illumination, and verification are the phases not just of my creative process, but of my entire life up to this point. And if that holds true for me—perfectly standard-issue as I am in terms of temperament, insecurities, desires, aspirations, and self-delusion—it must certainly hold true for others, very much including those who are not leading "artistic" lives. In other words, if we observe in our lives the same sequential development outlined by Gordon for the production of a work of art, our lives in effect become one protracted creative process, of which we ourselves—our selves—are the product. We are the creators of our selves, and our selves are our work. Creator and creation, artist and artwork, in one not-so-neat package.

Simple, no?

Nancy had met Nick briefly once before, in the summer of '72, when she was fourteen. She had stayed behind in London to attend the summer session of the National Youth Theatre while the rest of us went on vacation to Italy with our dad. Nick was a friend of our male nanny, Phil, who had asked him to look in on Nancy while we were gone, so Nick and his girlfriend, Cherry, had taken her out to the Hard Rock Café, where she had the number seven, a burger with barbecue sauce. The evening didn't make much of an impression on her; Nick and Cherry were eighteen—grown-ups—and Nancy didn't have much use for grown-ups at her age.

But three years later, sometime in the winter of '75, Nancy decided to throw a dinner party with her friends Nicky and Louise and a number of others. It was going to be all girls and it was going to be very elegant: avocado vinaigrette with shrimp, spaghetti bolognese, green salad, garlic bread, chocolate mousse. The girls were all dressed up in their finest, drinking Chianti from fiascoes, when Phil came home after seeing *Romeo and Juliet* at the cinema with his friend Nick. With his blow-dried hair parted down the middle, his wide-flared jeans, checked shirt, and oxblood leather platform boots, Nick was the most gorgeous man Nancy had ever seen. He lowered his chin and cocked his head when he smiled at you, as if you were a golf ball. At that moment, my brother Scott showed up with his rowdy friends for the weekly ritual of watching *Match of the Day* on the television, and the party broke up. Nicky and Louise stayed the night; Nick slept over too, sharing Phil's room next door to Nancy's. All the girls were smitten. They stayed up all night talking and giggling about the beautiful man just the other side of the wall.

Not long after, Nick invited Nancy and his own sister Pru down to a party in Redhill, south of London, where he had just started working as a driller for British Industrial Sand. During the course of the party he sat with his arm around Nancy, which to her was the same as saying that he was in love with her. Later, he drove her to the station for the train back to the city, stopping off to buy licorice cuttings, which were his favorite. As he saw her off, Nick told Nancy casually that he'd call her sometime, which even she knew meant that he might never call. She didn't care. She was in love.

But he did call, and they went on a date, again to the Hard Rock. Nick's impressive title at BSI was geological field technician; he was a regular at the Hard Rock and he knew the maître d', so they got the VIP treatment. Nancy ordered the number seven again and a piece of devil's food cake, but she couldn't eat any of it. Not long after, Nick invited her back to Redhill. At some point in the evening, with Nick's arm around her shoulder, Nancy said, "So what do you think?" and Nick answered "I think we could have a few laughs together." It was March 27, 1975, just shy of her seventeenth birthday. It's all in her diary.

The early to mid-1970s were not a good time in the story of our family. In 1970, my father, a commercial artist and graphic designer, had accepted a job at an ad agency in London, and had moved us all there into a sprawling Victorian duplex apartment in the shadow of Westminster Cathedral— four children, ages fourteen to five, and my mother, who had only recently been diagnosed with multiple sclerosis and was already walking with a cane. My parents split up in 1971, less than a year after the move, and my father moved out, living in a series of tiny apartments all over the city, where we saw him on the weekends whenever possible. He had just come out as a gay man and needed time to understand and grow into his new identity. We lived with our mother, who was then in her late thirties; as the multiple sclerosis progressed, she became increasingly unable to care for herself, going from cane to wheelchair to bedridden within a span of just three years. For an extended period before she was finally compelled to move to a nursing home, we children largely ran the household, including feeding our mother and helping her on the toilet and in the bath. We had a series of live-in nannies, some competent and kind, others neither one nor the other, of whom Phil was but the latest and least qualified, but not necessarily the worst. None stayed for very long in any case.

For the most part, we children were left to our own devices. By the time I was thirteen, I already had a healthy drinking habit and was beginning to experiment with drugs, although I was and remained a good student and an avid reader. As the youngest, Jenny and I were most often thrown together; I tortured her mercilessly, but it was also me who took her to school every day, to the dentist and the doctor when she needed treatment, and to the hospital whenever our mother came down with a bout of the recurrent pneumonia that would eventually kill her. Nancy did her best to give Jenny a little of the mothering that she so desperately needed, but like Scott, Nancy was an independent teenager at the beginning of her own journey, crazy for the stage and desperate to escape the misery and claustrophobia of our home, and often unavailable. It was against the backdrop of this grim scenario that she fell in love with Nick.

"Essential to and underlying the creative process is the search for meaning." It's never easy and often impossible to know what people mean when they use the word "meaning." Usually, I think, they aren't terribly certain themselves. Just as anyone can cook a chicken but cooking a chicken really well is the test of a great chef, so too is it easy enough to drop the word "meaning" into your conversation, but it is extremely rare that any of us truly knows how to make the best use of it. I myself have used it in that lazy, nebulous manner earlier in this book—"those whose guiding light is the search for meaning in our lives"—trusting to the reader to fill in the blanks.

Because Rosemary Gordon died in 2012, we may well never know what she meant by it. She shares with us her conviction that it "evolves out of a synthesis of the process of differentiation and ordering on the one hand and the making and discovering of something new on the other," and likewise that it is "inseparable from the capacity for awe and wonder and from the courage to be genuinely available to any kind of experience," but we still don't know what it *means*. Yet it was clearly of the highest importance to her, since she used it in the subtitle of her book, and she asserts on the very first page of chapter one that "only those who can look death squarely in the face can really live a meaningful life." So right from the beginning we know that, whatever "meaning" may be, it is a matter of life and death. And that seems reasonable to me, since by any practical interpretation of the word no one who is indifferent to the search for meaning can be said to be truly alive.

When you sign on to believing in God, you get your meaning of life as an added bonus, but those of us who don't believe are looking for something, too, and often just as desperately. But just because there is no answer when you cry "Why am I here?" into the void doesn't mean you can't legitimately ask the question. You just have to answer it yourself, like an existentialist. And there's no point looking for yours in places where others have been lucky enough to find theirs, but once you do start searching you soon come to see that you had been searching for it long before you were conscious of searching for it, so you know that, whatever *it* is, that is what "meaning" means. And you will know what it means once you find it. In a certain sense, it could be said that the whole purpose of this book is a search for the meaning of the word "meaning."

Nick and Nancy began seeing each other. When he was in London, Nick would pick her up in front of her school in his Land Rover and Ray-Ban aviator sunglasses. He came by our apartment often. He was handsome and funny and generous, and he treated me far more indulgently than Phil, who was often short-tempered and abusive. I was thirteen; for me, Nick represented something new—strength, confidence, freedom. I knew exactly why Nancy was in love with him because I loved him for the same reasons. Where I had precocity, books, and humor to keep reality at bay, he had strong opinions and was not afraid to use them. Where I had strong drugs, he seems to have had an even stronger moral compass. I was afraid of everything, and he was afraid of nothing and no one. I immediately adopted him as a role model and protector against Phil.

He got to be good friends with Scott, and they decided that they were going to travel together that summer. Over the Easter holiday, the BBC had filmed a National Youth Theatre drama in which Nancy had played the role of a terrorist named Shona and had built a bomb onstage. On the day it was to air, the whole family, including Nick, gathered around the TV to watch. Nancy, Jenny, and my father were all having their hair permed by the hairdresser, who did house calls, and the air was thick with the stench of sulfur. Nick said to my father, "Don't you think it would be a good idea if I moved in so I could get to know Scott better?" So he moved in and spent the summer with us before he and Scott set off to hitch-hike through Europe to Greece in the fall.

For some time, Nancy had been planning to leave London to complete her last two years of schooling in the drama and liberal arts program at South Warwickshire College of Further Education, in Stratford-on-Avon. The program culminated, as did all high schools, in the college-entry exams known as the A-levels, after which Nancy planned on applying to drama school. It was a highly regarded course and unique in England at the time, so Nancy was thrilled to be accepted. She had attended the National Academy of Ballet in New York before we moved to the United Kingdom, and she had even been a little swan onstage with the Bolshoi at the Met during its first-ever visit to the United States, in 1968, but circumstances had compelled her to drop ballet, and ever since she had focused all her ambition and passion on acting. In addition to summers at the National Youth Theatre, she had attended drama classes in West Hampstead every Saturday since the age of twelve. She says now that what she loved most about being in the theatre was not so much the performance as the rehearsal process, the team-building and camaraderie, the family feeling, the relationships, much of which was lacking in our home at that time. "I've never had discipline like that in my life; the way they ran us through our paces. It was like living with a big family." Ours, too, was a big family, but that's obviously not how she meant it.

But in Stratford, she pined for Nick, and when his trip with Scott was cut short because he, too, was miserable without her, she began to hitchhike back and forth to London every weekend just to be with him, and her studies suffered.

At the end of the year, with only two terms left before her exams, Nick asked Nancy to leave school so they could be together all the time. Everybody without exception told her it would be a terrible mistake, and she herself felt sick to her stomach at the thought of it, because she knew it was wrong, but she dismissed her feelings as relics of conventional thinking. Nick's way was the road less traveled, and she wanted to travel it with him. Still, she spent the summer hoping that something, anything, would somehow change, that she could find a way to back out of the decision, before she had to inform the program director—or that the school would burn down so she wouldn't have to. Our father was reluctant to allow it but ultimately did not stand in her way. She didn't even try very hard to justify herself because there really was no justification; all she knew was that she wanted to be with Nick and Nick wanted her all to himself. He was the first person who had ever paid exclusive attention to her, and he could not bear to share her attention and care with anyone or anything. Let other people have their educations, their careers, their communities of friends and confidants. She had Nick.

To move and to change means to accept awareness of our approaching end. But to refuse to change means being dead now.

—ROSEMARY GORDON

The next ten years for Nancy were a blur of aimless wandering, odd jobs, constant penury and money worries, and fathomless self-denial. But they were also an adventure. At one point she and Nick lived on a river barge on the Thames, right around the corner from the Royal Academy ballet school, which served only to remind her that all her friends were away at college. After living on the barge, the couple took jobs as servants on an estate in Hampshire, Nancy as a maidservant to the lady of the house, Nick as a handyman. They returned to London when our mother died in 1976, but Nick soon grew restless again and they decided to try their luck in America; they married so Nick could get his green card. They moved to White Plains, just north of New York City, to live with my mother's sister Harriet until they got on their feet. Living at Harriet's felt to Nancy like coming home, or even going back to a safer, more orderly, and predictable time. She found a job she loved, working for the Conran design company, and even had hopes to enroll in the well-regarded drama program at the nearby Purchase campus of the state university. But then Nick decided that they should move to Newport, Rhode Island, where he had a distant cousin. It was January, Newport was freezing, and their house had no heat. Nick contracted pneumonia and Nancy found work waitressing at a diner. Over the next few months they moved so many times that Nancy lost track. At one point they moved in with

Nancy's friend Rita, until one night Nick confessed that he and Rita were having an affair and he didn't know how to extricate himself from it. He and Nancy made their escape in a midnight flit.

Gradually, however, things seemed like they were settling down. She loved her job at the diner and was asked to join the Rhode Island Shakespeare Theater. She made close friends and was able for once to stick around long enough to nurture the friendships. Nick borrowed a library book on picture framing and bluffed his way into a job at an art gallery. Framing is a solitary, meticulous craft, and Nick proved to be a natural. Over the years, he would hone his craft and become a fine art framer and gilder, culminating in a brief stint at the Royal Academy of Arts in London. But no matter what he managed to accomplish, none of it was able to satisfy his need to keep moving. Nick had a sharp and inquiring mind and a decent education; he was well read and had ambitions as an artist and a writer, but he had no confidence in himself and was mostly unable to capitalize on any of his skills. Instead, he seemed perpetually determined to undermine every opportunity to build on any success he might enjoy or to establish the kind of stable working and emotional environment and relationships in which he could begin to face down the demons that plagued him. And through it all—the affairs, the angry silences and storming rages, the possessive jealousy, the endless pinballing among Newport, London, New York, San Francisco—Nancy stuck with him and weathered the storms as best she could.

At that point, all hope of returning to the theater was dead, and she began to tell herself what she would tell herself for decades: "I'll just wait until Nick's sorted out and then I'll go back to my life." It was not as if she were being held captive; she wanted to be with him more than anything, but she also wanted him to be different and thought he could fulfill his creative potential if only he could overcome his inner turmoil. That, more than anything, was why she stayed. In the meantime, her existence was a study in appeasement. One day in Newport, she ran into Rita, her former friend who had had the affair with Nick. "You must hate me," Rita said. "I don't hate you," Nancy told her. "I just want you and Nick to be friends again." Compliance and fear of conflict had by that time become the standard operating procedure for her. It's almost impossible to believe that, after all she'd been through, she was still only twenty-one years old at that point. She had already learned everything there is to know about self-effacement. Waiting for Nick to change, she was unable to grow and change herself. It was what Rosemary Gordon might have called a refusal to change, a kind of psychic death in life.

Ever since the day she had agreed to drop out of high school, she had been plagued by a chronic feeling of butter-flies in her stomach, a sense of what she calls "pathological nostalgia"—a creeping, debilitating hankering to go back-ward, to find a real home—that lasted for decades. Yet she did not feel capable of looking after herself. "He would say that I was an impediment, that I was a child, that I was dependent, but he also didn't allow me to grow up. I didn't know how to be grown-up or a woman with him. It was a collusion that worked for us both on some level."

This unsettled, unsettling life went on for several years. At one point, Nick took a break in San Francisco, where he stayed with my father, who had left England the year before with Jenny and me. Nancy was left alone in Newport. She recalls those months by herself as among the happiest of her life. She bought a pink princess phone with an illuminated dial, of the sort she had seen in American teen movies when we had lived in England. I stayed with her that summer on my way to college in upstate New York. I remember how happy she was, and how girlish and perky with her princess phone and her ersatz, belated American adolescence. But it didn't last long; in San Francisco, Nick decided that he needed to be with her again. After a passionate but rather foolhardy reunion, Nancy discovered that she was pregnant. They had a brief discussion in which Nancy made it very clear that she did not want and was not ready for this baby. She took a bus on her own to a Boston clinic and they never talked about it again. She now recognizes that this may have been her first act of independence. She had done it for herself, and not for him.

She hadn't even really wanted him to come back—she'd felt exactly the same as she had when she'd left school, as if her life were over—but she wasn't strong enough to say no. Asked if she was still in love with him at that point, she says: "Whatever that means. He was all I knew really. I knew it wasn't right but I couldn't give him up. I kind of thought that we were living this Bloomsbury Set life, that we were open and liberal, and it was all a question of 'I don't care what he does as long as he comes back to me.' " She says that they were more like brother and sister at this point, but she still desperately wanted a romantic relationship with him. This was a pattern that was to be repeated again and again over the years. Nick would wear Nancy down, undermining her self-confidence, accusing her of being unattractive and babyish and committed to nothing. At the same time, what he really seemed to want was for her to be committed exclusively to him, not to want anything for herself. He felt that if she had friends and interests outside the couple, she wasn't committed to him; he took any failure to focus exclusively on him as a personal betrayal. "I believed everything he said. I thought I was as bad as he said I was. I didn't know any different." In the meantime, she protected their relationship quite convincingly, and even people who knew her very well would later say they had no idea she had been so unhappy—largely, she claims, because a big part of her didn't know she was unhappy.

In 1983, Nancy and I wound up in New York City at the same time, right after my graduation from college, and I moved into her studio apartment on Avenue C. She joined a children's theater company and took Method acting classes at the HB Studio. The Method requires the actor to plumb the depths of her psyche in order to understand a character and bring authenticity to a role, but Nancy struggled, she now realizes, because she had no idea who she was. She could not find that part of herself and wasn't even convinced that it existed. Nick was in London, engaged in yet another affair, but eventually he joined us and we lived together very happily on the Lower East Side for a couple of years. It wasn't always bad, or all bad, and that was part of the problem.

Nick had extreme and sometimes frightening—though never violent—mood swings, and you never knew what would upset his sense of moral balance. He could go ballistic at a moment's notice, especially if he thought you were being disingenuous or somehow untrue to your own beliefs, and he had little tolerance for idle chitchat. But these were also the qualities that made his company so compelling, when he was "up," because he never stopped thinking or questioning, and he could be adorably silly and funny when the mood was on him. He was a lot like John Lennon, whom he greatly admired and unconsciously emulated, right down to the quirky doodling. As a boy, I had worshipped him for all these reasons, and an element of that worship endured even when he lost his temper and even, later, when I'd just had enough and was exhausted by his volatility. I was convinced even then that he had a direct tap into a deep well of moral truth that fueled his bitter intolerance of hypocrisy and self-deceit. There always seemed to be a nugget of truth in what he said, which was what made it so easy to take it on board. He was capable of exploding if he suspected that you were being dishonest with yourself. For instance, at a later stage in our friendship, if I happened to complain about my frustrations with my job, he would fly off the handle, accusing me of being weak and craven for not simply walking away from it all if I was unhappy. Of course, it was in large part his example of walking away from all his problems, and all the unhappiness left in his wake when he did, that kept me where I was, even if I felt that there was a core of painful, necessary honesty in what he said.

In the spring of 1985, my friend Guy went to scout real estate in southwestern France, where there were amazing deals to be had, and he asked me to come along to translate. We traveled extensively in the Aude and Ariège, whose tiny villages had been emptied by the flight of young people to the cities, and it was true—you could find modest but lovely old stone houses in these hamlets for next to nothing, especially with the franc at ten or eleven to the dollar. On my return to New York, Nancy and Nick grew very excited at the prospect of owning a little house in the south of France, and in June Nick and I returned. After less than two weeks, we found just what we were looking for in the tiny village of Bellegarde-du-Razès, a typical Languedoc *circulade* built in a snail-shell pattern at the top of a hill to defend against marauding armies in the early Middle Ages. Our house had thirteenth-century foundations and views all the way to the Pyrenees. We first saw it at 6:00 p.m.; by noon the next day, we had struck a deal to buy it for twelve thousand dollars cash. We put down a two-thousand-dollar deposit and promised to return in three months with the rest.

By this time, I had already been offered my fellowship at Northwestern, and it didn't make much sense for me to be a third owner in the house, as originally planned, but Nancy and Nick worked their asses off for three months and somehow put together the remaining ten thousand dollars. They made it to Bellegarde just in time to join the grape harvest, which was good timing, as they did not have a penny left to their name. When Nancy saw the house, even with no furniture and its bare concrete floors, she knew it was the home she had been looking for all these years.

Grape harvesting is not for the faint of heart. It is grueling work, and Nick and Nancy were the only pickers who were not peasants or migrant workers. The labor and hours were brutal, and Nancy soon began to flag, but the money was good and they couldn't afford to pass it up. Even when she could barely stand she worked twelve hours a day, then went back to the house to strip wallpaper. When she got a blister on her thumb that wouldn't heal, she had to walk the three kilometers and back to the neighboring village, in the scorching heat, to see the doctor. He gave her some penicillin and asked her to come back the next day for a blood test, and again she had to go on foot. That night there was a knock at their door. Nancy thought it was her coworker Mohammed, who sometimes stopped in for a shower before visiting his girlfriend, but it was Dr. Dufont, who told her that she had to go to the hospital—not at the end of the harvest but immediately, the very next morning.

> *The moment of blankness and extinction can become, if recognised and accepted, the moment of incipient fruitfulness, and that acceptance of death is truly the final test of the acceptance of reality.*
>   —ROSEMARY GORDON

Nancy was under continuous sedation for the next few days, and she doesn't remember much. She and Nick got a lift to Purpan Hospital in Toulouse, where she was given a platelet transfusion and a sternum puncture. She was then stretchered onto a commercial flight to Gatwick; Nick had to prop her up in a sitting position the whole way because of the squeezing pain around her heart. She was ambulanced to Saint Bart's Hospital, near the Smithfield Market in London, where my father was already waiting for her. She still had no idea what was wrong with her. Today, she can't for the life of her remember how she could have failed to ask; even when she was placed in a ward full of leukemia patients, her only thought was one of sympathy for their suffering. She also remembers the joy of receiving her first and only towel bath on her first night. It wasn't until Dr. Lister, the head of the oncology unit, came around the next day to tell her she was suffering from acute myeloid leukemia and had a week to live that it began to sink in.

She spent the next three months in that old, high-ceilinged Victorian ward of twelve beds, where the nurses wore starched wimples and sat at your side and held your hand when you were feeling low. She was treated with bright-red Adriamycin, administered in massive syringes until her veins gave out, at which point she had a shunt surgically implanted into her chest for ease of administration. Her treatment also included numerous painful bone marrow punctures in the back of her pelvis. She soon learned the unspoken rules and customs observed by the patients. She viewed their ward as the "road" they lived on; the geriatrics lived on the road next door, but the women on the leukemia ward never ventured that way. Patients were allowed to smoke in the hallways and to go to the pub at night, although Nancy took her treatment seriously and never did such things. She learned how to sleep through breakfast by staying up very late, padding around the ward in her slippers, washing the dishes in the kitchen and making tea for the nurses, stealing sweets from the sleeping patients, and watching classic films on the television.

She began to ally herself with the nurses, offering up her services, whether it was holding a drip stand or a bag of blood, or being their ear in the middle of the night when they wanted to talk about their troubles, romances, and issues with senior doctors. She also became a sort of unofficial counselor to her fellow patients. The nurses would say, "Oh, Joyce is a bit sad, would you go talk to her, Nancy?" and mothers would ask her to talk to their daughters and persuade them to try her healthy lifestyle. Even Dr. Lister once asked her to pop her head into a favorite patient's room; she thought he had done so just to make her feel useful, but afterward he thanked her profusely for her help. Being useful gave her a purpose and a defense against acknowledging her own problems, fears, and above all needs, but she also resented it at times and plaintively wrote in her diary, "Why isn't there someone on the ward like me *for* me?" To this day, she still feels a powerful pull and at times an overriding imperative to attend to others rather than to herself.

The bed at the top of the ward near the nurses' station was the scary one; if you got moved up there you knew your days were numbered. Everybody understood what it meant when the curtains of a cubicle were not just drawn but held tightly shut with safety pins. The staff would wait for the cover of night to cart off the dead woman in a steel sarcophagus, and by morning her bed had been fully stripped, sponged, and sanitized. Most of the women on the ward had died by the time Nancy was declared in remission in February and sent

home, which for the moment was a basement flat that Nick
had rented on Fulham Palace Road. For the next year or so,
Nick really shouldered his responsibilities with uncharac-
teristic reliability, holding down a steady job at a high-end
framing shop in Chelsea, buying a car, and ensuring that
Nancy ate nothing but whole foods.

The first order of business while her hair grew back was
to learn how to take care of herself in this new world of cancer recovery. She spent two weeks in the Bristol Cancer Centre, a progressive facility that combined traditional medicine
with therapy and alternative, non-Western programs, such as
meditation and macrobiotics. She found the regimen quite
rigorous and not entirely to her taste, but the food was deli-
cious and she appreciated the newfound privacy after months
on an open ward. She was also deeply affected and intrigued
by her introduction to psychotherapy there. She continued to
see a therapist after she returned to London, but found that
the psychosynthesis practiced in Bristol, which was heavily
based on imagery and required a level of imagination and
creativity that she had not yet recovered following her illness,
did not suit her. She wanted talking therapy. She began to
read and look into the alternatives, and gradually—with the
memory of the help she had offered her fellow patients in
the hospital still fresh in her mind—she realized that it was
in-depth psychotherapy that interested her, not counseling.
She found a wonderful psychotherapist in Camden who not
only helped her with her own issues but also encouraged her
to consider how to further her understanding of and involvement in the process.

The following fall, slightly less than a year since her diagnosis, Nancy underwent her bone marrow transplant. The state-of-the-art transplant unit was in Sutton, in the southern suburbs of London. By an incredible stroke of good luck, Jenny and I were both compatible donors, but Jenny was chosen because she was the same sex as Nancy. While Jenny had bone marrow harvested from her pelvis with a syringe the size of her forearm, Nancy underwent total body irradiation, killing all the bone marrow in her body, and with it her entire immune system. She spent the next four weeks in an isolation bubble, with human contact limited to hospital staff in hazmat suits, waiting while every last white blood cell died off and then, with unbearable and rising tension, to see whether the transplant had taken. It took three days from the time her T cell count fell to zero until the first tiny upswing indicating that the new marrow was alive and productive. After that, her stem cell count rose little by little every day, restoring her immune system.

Nancy's months at Saint Bart's had been wonderfully productive in terms of writing letters, keeping her journals, doing her needlework, and counseling her fellow patients, and she had been looking forward to more of the same in her luxurious "isolation suite" at Sutton following the transplant, but the only facilities she had any use for were the toilet and the bucket. It was, in her words, "horrible horrible horrible and a very weird feeling." She was extremely weak and suffered from headaches, nausea, and diarrhea all the time. The graft-versus-host disease, which is expected and even desired in transplant patients, felt like tiny insects crawling under her skin and in her hair. With chemo, she had lost only the hair on her head. With the transplant, she had no hair left anywhere on her body by the time she was sent home, and she weighed ninety-five pounds.

> *My initial stay in hospital was pivotal for me because I finally got the rest and care that I desperately needed. All responsibility was taken away from me. I didn't have to feel guilty about Nick anymore even though I did; I felt as though I'd ruined his life, but for once what was going on for me was more important than what was going on for anyone else, including him, so I just relaxed and I let people look after me. It was like everything I needed the last ten years had been building to that point. Something would've happened to me, that's all I'm saying . . . I'm not glad I had it, but it would've been something else that would've cracked me open to start whatever life I was going to have, and it just happened to be this.*

The recovery was far worse than the treatment. She describes it like the grief you feel on the death of a loved one. "There's lots to do prior to the funeral and the will and all of that, but when everyone goes home and the wake is over you're left, and that's what it was like for me coming home. I was absolutely terrified and I was so fragile, unlike before." She spent the next couple of years in a kind of daze, as if she were waiting to be born again, but not in a good, embrace-every-day-the-rest-of-her-life way. Her life had become her illness. All the fear and all the depression that she had managed to marginalize, not only through her illness but for many years before that, began to push themselves to the fore, and there

were days, she says, when she didn't know how she would
manage. There was a disconnect between her mind and her
body, "like when you see footage of the spaceship detaching
from the engine and then the capsule goes off on its own . . .
I just felt not in touch with reality a lot of the time, I developed some very strange phobias." She experienced a total loss
of creativity and spontaneity. She couldn't read or write; she
couldn't even cook without following an exact recipe. That's
what anxiety is, she says; it's not about dying, it's about being
in touch with having nearly died.

She was still desperately weak—for the first few months
she could barely move—but she felt so beholden and so responsible to Nick that she tidied the house and had dinner
ready for him when he came home every night. They didn't
have a refrigerator or even an oven, just a hot plate, and Nick
slowly furnished the apartment with chipboard furniture he
built himself. The way they'd been living for all those years,
never planning further than the next time they'd run out
of money so long as they could get away with it, suddenly all
felt so impermanent and tentative. This new reality was the
future now: thirty-six drugs a day, blood tests twice a week,
forbidden to use public transportation for fear of infections,
five years until she was declared cured if she got that far, recurring health issues for the rest of her life.

After a few months she went back to work, after a fashion, part-time for a medical charity run by our dear friend
Shannie Ross. Nancy knew that she was not up to even a me-
nial job, but Shannie coddled and mothered her and restored
a little sense of her self-worth. "I couldn't have done much

more at the time. My confidence had been absolutely knocked out of me. I was not like a baby but like a different person; somewhere that was me in there. It took a long time to come out."

At this point, they were living in Muswell Hill, a suburb on the northern fringes of London, and with her travel restrictions Nancy was quite isolated. Nick had begun behaving oddly again, and she suspected that he was probably seeing somebody. They decided that he would move out, and the ensuing separation of five months was the longest they'd lived apart in fifteen years, although he eventually set up a workshop in the flat for his framing business, so they would see each other during the day when she wasn't working. Jenny came to live with her for a while, too. It was at that point that they agreed to begin divorce proceedings, not because they planned to remain apart but because they thought it might help, even save their relationship. The divorce came through in 1988, by which time they were back together.

The following year they decided that it might be best for Nancy's health if they were to leave the city. They found a house in the little Gloucestershire village of Mickleton, not far from where Nick had grown up. He set up a framing business and went about cultivating the wealthy weekenders and landed gentry of the Vale of Evesham. Nancy continued to work two or three days a week for the charity in London, staying sometimes with Jenny, sometimes with Shannie. She was also thinking seriously, perhaps for the first time in her adult life, about her future. Organically and in a piecemeal sort of fashion over the course of several years, the outlines of a possible new direction and purpose had begun to fall into place. She had been pursuing her research into psychotherapy for some time, and she had started to mine the directories published by the United Kingdom Council for Psychotherapy for information about training programs. She knew that, without a college degree and having failed even to finish high school, the odds were against finding any accredited institution that would accept her, but she felt that this was what she wanted to do with her life. It was in Mickleton that she celebrated the five-year "all clear" date that officially marked her as cured.

One of Nick's customers was a well-heeled London transplant who lived with her husband and children in a manor house on a farm owned by her brother-in-law, a very wealthy member of the landed gentry. When the lease on the house in Mickleton lapsed, this woman suggested that Nick and Nancy might like to move into one of the eighteenth-century Cotswold stone cottages on the farm, where a vacant barn-and-stable compound could be converted into a workshop for Nick and an art gallery that she and Nick would run as equal partners. Both Nick and Nancy jumped at this opportunity, and their tenure on the farm began very hopefully, even though Nancy still did not have her driver's license and was completely dependent on Nick for transportation.

It was shortly after their move that Nancy's perseverance paid off, and she was offered a place in the foundation course at the Minster Centre in London, an integrative psychotherapy training institute that was willing to accept her life experience in lieu of academic qualifications. In the autobiographical essay that she had written as part of her application, she had been asked to explain why she wanted to train and why she was drawn to psychotherapy, and this exercise had focused her thinking on her own experiences and traumas. She had come to believe that everything that had happened to her in the ten years before she fell ill—and even earlier, going back to the death of our mother, which had been largely swept under the carpet in our family and was hardly ever discussed or addressed among us—was a critical or at least a contributing factor of her disease. In some way, the toxic stresses of her life, and her failure ever to express or even acknowledge them, had poisoned and sickened her. The germ of this idea had been born when she was in the hospital, and it had grown slowly and organically ever since. It had also been in the hospital that Nancy had finally begun to mourn the loss of our mother and to acknowledge how terrified and isolated she must have felt, so her training to become a psychotherapist was about more than wanting to help others who had suffered as she had; it was about wanting to give something back, and it was about wanting to explore, understand, and heal herself more deeply. The two therapists who had interviewed her at the Minster Centre had been incredibly warm and empathetic. They had really listened to her. They seemed to see something in her that she herself had been barely aware of. They made it clear that her life experience was important and validating. Nancy was thirty-three when she began her training—fifteen years after she had dropped out of high school to follow Nick.

Paying for school was going to be a problem, and it would

remain so throughout her six years at the Minster Centre (including one year when she had to suspend her studies for lack of funds). She got a job as an administrative assistant in Oxford, some twenty-five miles from the farm, at the Workers' Educational Association, which helped with a substantial loan. She would remain at the WEA for the next fourteen years, long after her accreditation, until she was able to support herself fully through psychotherapy. Once a week, and sometimes on weekends, she took the train to London for her coursework. As a therapist-in-training, she was also required to be in therapy herself, which somehow had to be paid for as well. Still, her first year at the Minster Centre was transformative, and it reaffirmed her instinct that this was what she wanted to do with the rest of her life. It also helped her to see a strong connection between acting and psychotherapy—which she had always experienced as a creative process—and so, for the first time, she saw that there might be a unifying thread of meaning and purpose in her life that she had never recognized before.

She can't quite remember when she learned that Nick and his partner were carrying on an affair, although she thinks it may have begun even before they had moved onto the farm. She suspects that everybody else knew all about it, but that she was in denial just as she had been when she had first fallen ill and had refused to ask what was wrong with herself. Before they moved in, he had told her that she didn't need to pay rent anymore because she had her school fees to cover. At the time, she thought that was a really generous offer, but in retrospect she came to see it as a ruthless way of easing her out of his life and appeasing his own guilt.

Only a few weeks after the move, and with Nancy's reluctant approval, Nick sold a half-share in their beloved Bellegarde house to his partner; in time (and against her will) he also sold his half of his and Nancy's remaining ownership, leaving Nancy with only a quarter share in the home she loved beyond words—and the only home she had ever owned. Suffice it to say, things were not good between them. She began to feel as if she were being replaced. Nick spent more and more time at the gallery or on trips with his lover, scouting out painters to represent. At home, they lived very separate lives; they no longer shared a bedroom, and Nick increasingly behaved as if Nancy didn't live there at all. Even then, however, she never challenged him or asked questions. She believed still that she was nothing without Nick, and she took him at his word when he told her that she didn't know how to be a grown-up. As the century drew to a close, they barely had any good moments together.

Nancy completed her training and in 1998 qualified to treat patients under supervision. She began to build a small practice in Oxford, alongside her job at the WEA, and to rent consulting rooms that she could barely afford. A friend of hers, who also commuted to Oxford from the Cotswolds, had rented a studio apartment in town where Nancy saw her patients, and she often stayed the night there rather than go all the way back to the farm. Slowly, she accumulated the clinical hours she needed in order to register.

It all came to a head in 2002. In May of that year, Nancy finally passed her driving test. When she called Nick from the car to tell him the news, there was a brief but telling pause before he congratulated her. Although Nick had always held it against her that she was so dependent on him, her growing independence over the years of her training had clearly weighed uneasily on him, and earning her driver's license seemed to clinch it. A few days later they had one of the nastiest and most vitriolic arguments they had ever had, and Nick said things that left little doubt about where he stood. She packed a very small bag, put it in the ancient, beat-up Volkswagen Golf that her friend Anne had given her, and left the next morning for work as usual. Nick rang her during the week to ask if she'd like to meet for Chinese food in Woodstock on her way home on Wednesday. She said she wasn't coming back on Wednesday. What about Thursday, he asked. She said she wasn't coming back at all. She did not return for over a year, and even then only to collect some of her books and pictures.

Nancy lived and worked in the studio flat for two years. She loved it there, but it was a very difficult time for her. She was full of rage, bitterness, jealousy, and a great sense of loss. When they had been together, Nick was always implying that she was holding him back and ruining his life, but whenever they broke up it had always been he who had come back to her. Or he would call for her advice about what he should do with his love life. As far back as their days on the Lower East Side, he would sometimes lie down on the bed and ask her to counsel him. With every affair, she told herself "Yes, but he always comes back to me." She had kept thinking that it was going to get better because she loved him. Her fear of leaving Nick had been connected to the fact that she continued to feel so grateful to be with such a gorgeous, talented, and unique man, and she was just waiting for his potential to flower.

But now that she was on her own in the studio, and her gratitude for being with him had finally and irrevocably worn out, she assumed that her life was about to go down the tubes while Nick, free of her at long last, would flourish and prosper among his sophisticated new clientele and friends, and that he would find the success and freedom that he'd always wanted.

In fact, the exact opposite occurred. The year 2003 was a pivotal one in Nancy's life. She went back into therapy, which helped her understand the dynamics of her relationship with Nick in a way she never had and to move on with her life. Within two years she was able to trade in the studio for the beautiful little flat that she still occupies in a quiet, leafy part of Oxford only minutes from the bucolic Port Meadow. The move launched what she describes as the most productive period of her entire life. She sold her remaining quarter-share in the Bellegarde house to Nick's partner. She started seeing someone. For ten years now, she's built her practice and professional reputation from strength to strength. A beloved and much respected tutor recommended her for a teaching job at the Minster Centre, where she now runs the first-year program. She says that this new responsibility somehow feels as if some kind of circle were closing. It feels, somehow, like a homecoming.

Creation depends . . . on the continuous interaction of life and death, of activity and passivity, of consciousness and unconsciousness, of assertion and surrender.

—ROSEMARY GORDON

In earlier chapters, I've used minibiographies to illuminate something about me, about how I interpret other people's lives to palliate some neurosis or insecurity I entertain about myself, or to help me understand what may be holding me back, preventing me from changing—in the hope, of course, that my findings would resonate with at least some of my readers. With Nancy's story, I've tried to escape that dynamic. I've tried to provide a straightforward life history, without slant or overt interpretation, that illustrates a genuine triumph over both external vicissitude and the internal shackles with which we unwittingly burden ourselves to slow our own progress. To me, Nancy's life is the rare and exemplary story of someone who has met the challenge of looking death squarely in the face and, as someone who is equally attuned to the "life forces" and the "death forces," has allowed the encounter to unleash the process of change that she had refused for decades. Nancy's experience of being mired in that state of refusal is an extreme instance, but it is one that we all recognize in one way or the other. None of us wants to change, because changing is hard work and an uncertain investment; we usually do it only when a crisis compels us to do it. Like Nancy, we sometimes need to be cracked open to get the process rolling. As the celebrated Swiss psychologist Marie-Louise von Franz once wrote, "The actual process of individuation—the conscious coming-to-terms with one's own inner center (psychic nucleus) or Self—generally begins with a wounding of the personality."

In Nancy's case, the wound was a literal, physiological one, but for most of us, the process of killing off an old ego so that we can adopt one of greater relevance and utility to our quest for meaning has to be figurative. Thankfully, most of us don't have to go through what Nancy went through to reach that point; instead, in a certain way, we have to do it to ourselves, under our own steam and with only our own imaginations as our guide. We have to somehow carry ourselves to the conclusion that the change we seek—a change that is so hard to envision from the perspective of a moribund and debilitating ego-conscious that has not evolved since the very beginning of our search for self—can be effected only by an act of creative annihilation. Although I suspect that she might dispute this, Nancy took Rosemary Gordon's four stages of the creative process and applied them to her entire life—to rebuilding her sense of self. But in order to do so, in order to embark on that initial, preparatory "period of conscious concern and struggle," she had first to do away with the diseased ego that had anchored her to a perpetual state of unchanging. First, she had to recognize that it was sick and had to resolve to effect a change; then she had to put it out of its misery, and an ego—even a diseased one—rarely goes down without a fight; then she had to create herself a new one, with no guidelines or points of reference to help; and finally, she had to test out the new one to see if it was a healthy fit. And that, ultimately, is what we are all called on to do if we want to make the best use of our experience and maturity. Preparation, incubation, illumination, and verification. While most of us won't have a life-and-death moment to precipitate it, we still have to find the strength and courage to crack ourselves wide open, step out of that old, dead skin, and keep walking.

Home Is Where
the Ghosts Live

In Rainer Maria Rilke's famous poem "Archaic Torso of Apollo," the poet stands before an ancient statue that, despite being headless, dazzles him with the radiance of its gaze. The entire torso, from the "curved breast" to the "placid hips and thighs" to the "dark center where procreation flared," is suffused with brilliance. It is "looking" at him not with eyes but with its entire physical, temporal, and emotional being. Because it breathes with this ancient intelligence, the torso does not appear defaced; on the contrary, the stone seems to glow or dazzle like a star as it peers into the deepest recesses of the poet's soul. And knowing everything there is to know about him, it speaks. "You must change your life," it tells him.

It's not hard to picture the poet, with his high starched collar and thick, swept-back hair, standing awestruck before the ancient Miletan torso on display in the Louvre. His boss, the sculptor Auguste Rodin, had sent him out into the world with instructions to stop writing about his childhood and about love, and to start seeing the world with his own eyes. In the museum that day, he was on assignment, like a high school student, which makes the revelation all the more unexpected. Even as Rilke stands there, trying to *see* the torso as if with new eyes, it is the torso that is watching him, seeing him for who he is, judging him, condemning him. And although it is a ruin without head, eyes, limbs, or reproductive organs, Rilke is the one who is incomplete, unpotentiated.

What was it that the torso saw in young Rilke that prompted it to offer him such portentous advice? Of all the wisdom the headless torso had to share with him, of all the counsel it had to offer, why did it choose that message? If you or I were to walk into the Louvre tomorrow and were somehow able to see the torso as clearly as Rilke did that day, would it have the same message for us, or was it aimed specifically at Rilke? Of course, the trick to answering these questions is to understand what it was that Rilke was really looking at on that pedestal. The torso, clearly, was no statue at all—it was a mirror, and the voice rising up out of the millennia to tell Rilke that he must change his life was his own. And if the torso was a mirror, and Rilke was indeed seeing himself in its reflection, was he seeing himself as he was at that moment, as he would be in 2,500 years, or as he had been 2,500 years ago? As he would be if he changed his life, or as he would be if he didn't change his life?

In the movies, the drunk wakes up with a hangover yet again, stumbles into the bathroom, and is suddenly confronted by a face in the mirror that would appear to be his own, and that yet has a kind of clarity to it, like Rilke's torso, that allows him to see himself in a new light—the light of a truth about himself that he suppresses or is otherwise not apparent to him in the course of his normal day. It hardly matters if we know the "real" circumstances of Rilke's life at the moment he looks in that mirror, what it may have been about his life that he felt needed to be changed. His friends might have thought they knew what it was; his biographers may think they know, but that too is irrelevant. He may not even have known or understood it himself. All he could have known for certain was that, when he looked into the mirror, he found himself being rebuked by a voice that was remarkably like his own yet without an identifiable source.

I think it's fair to say that we have all found ourselves in Rilke's situation at one point in our lives or another. You don't have to be a poet, or an alcoholic, or even necessarily feel that your life is somehow terribly out of kilter, to be stopped short by that disembodied voice in your ear or that headless torso in the mirror. It was hearing that voice that first prompted me to question what I thought I understood about myself, about who I was, and ultimately to try to make sense of it all. It is this voice, more than my own, that is narrating the pages of that book. We've all heard this voice before. We don't know where it comes from, and we can't always make out what it is saying as clearly as Rilke was able to, but we recognize it as surely as we recognize our own faces in the mirror. One way or another, we all end up as ghosts haunting our own lives.

I could be wrong about this, but it seems to me that, until relatively recently, there was an unspoken consensus about what ghost stories were supposed to be. There are living people on one side, dead people on the other, and between them a barrier that is generally impermeable but that, in certain circumstances, can become porous. When that happens, the dead reach through or cross the barrier and seek to interact with the living. It is their various reasons for doing so that constitute the plots of ghost stories. Now, obviously there are exceptions to this template; I'm not trying to describe a rigid or unchanging formula, and I haven't made a rigorous study of any kind to back up my thesis. It's just a general impression of how most ghost stories work.

I'm not deeply read in the repertory of classic ghost stories, either, but I do enjoy a good ghost movie. Stanley Kubrick's *The Shining*, among others, is an apt illustration of the mechanics behind the kind of traditional ghost story I'm talking about, in which the dead, for reasons of their own that are not always clear to the living, reach across the membrane that divides the two worlds. Joe Mankiewicz's 1947 supernatural romance *The Ghost and Mrs. Muir* is another, just to demonstrate how different the stories can be even as they adhere to the same principle. However wide the variations in circumstance, the idea and archetype behind them all are essentially constant—the dead initiate the interaction because of some communication they need to share or some frustration (in the very broadest sense) they can satisfy only with the collusion of the living. In every case, it is the dead who are in some way incomplete, and the living who hold the key to their dilemma. Ghost stories tend to have a very biocentric perspective because they are always written by living people who seem to have a need to demonstrate their ultimate superiority over ghosts, despite the arsenal of paranormal and psychological weapons available to the dead against which the living have no defense. It's not unlike the classic neocolonial paradigm, with restless natives supplanted by restless souls. We have to dehumanize what we fear in order to defeat it.

But the paradigm seems to be changing. Again, I could be wrong, but as far as I can tell the shift began with the release of the film *The Sixth Sense*, directed by M. Night Shyamalan, in 1999. It is almost as if the ghosts, sick and tired of always being portrayed as needy and incomplete, had started to write ghost stories from their own perspective. To my mind, far and away the best representative of this new subgenre is the 2001 movie *The Others*, directed by Alejandro Amenábar and starring Nicole Kidman. In these movies and others like them, the plot pivots on a fundamental misunderstanding unwittingly embraced by the main characters—those who believe themselves to be alive, and to be haunted by ghosts, are actually dead, and the beings they had mistaken for ghosts turn out to be living people trying to communicate with them. The traditional relationship between living and dead is overturned, the vector of outreach and assistance reversed, and the very nature of the difference between the two states of being thrown into question. Reality turns out to be the opposite of what the protagonists thought it was, the haunter becomes the haunted, and it is difficult to determine which side of the boundary you are on. Those who believed themselves to be actors are in fact being acted upon by; the leaders become the led.

I couldn't say what it is about the zeitgeist that has sparked this shift, this new ghost-sensitive perspective, but I find it fascinating, among other reasons, because it seems to hold true of all the lives I've explored in this book, emphatically including my own. It is Rilke going to the museum to look at art, only to find that it is the art looking at him. The fact that none of us, one way or another, is precisely who he thinks he is, can, I hope, be taken for granted at this point. Most of us don't know who we are or where to look for this "self" we keep hearing about, and it is precisely when we imagine that we have achieved a certain understanding that we are most often mistaken because we still haven't figured out what we're looking for, what the thing we're looking for looks like, or even what purpose it might serve us to find it. Self-knowledge is neither a walking stick nor a road map; it is the distant landmark toward which we aim our steps, often only fitfully visible through fog or rain, and constantly shifting in shape, size, and apparent distance as our road twists and turns and our perspective changes. Often, like Dante, we find ourselves walking blind, in the dark, with only the vaguest sense of the direction we are supposed to take and no view whatsoever of our ultimate goal. We sometimes feel like ghosts in our own lives, semitransparent in the mirror and rattling our chains not to scare others but to comfort ourselves with evidence of our own existence. Still, so long as we choose to remain alive even as we stumble along in the gloom with our arms out-stretched and the foreboding that the walls are closing in on us, the sound of our faltering steps seems to remind us that we retain agency, that we continue to move ahead on our own power, and that we have thereby managed to maintain some sort of control, howsoever incoherent, over own destinies. Even when we can no longer see the ends of our own nose, we are convinced that those footsteps we hear are our own. Simply to be alive and to remain alive is to exercise free will, and we are the living.

But what if none of it were true, or rather, what if it were all based on a fundamental misreading of our own situations? What if we thought we were standing with our two feet on the ground when all the time we were actually hovering above it without a tether or ballast? Who's footfall is that we hear in the dark, if it's not our own? And if it isn't our own, and we have no idea what direction we're heading in, how can we tell if it's stalking us or leading us? What if, like A. D. Harvey, I am not a brilliant historian whose precocious career was smothered in the crib, but rather a paranoid narcissist who finds it easier to embrace conspiracy theories than the complexities of social intercourse? What if, like Jack Gilbert, I am not an iconoclastic poet who has developed a fierce honesty over a lifetime spent defending my independence from the vapid, venal world, but rather an insecure, judgmental misanthrope with no insight into the human condition? What if, like Kafka, I am constrained not by the shackles of bourgeois necessity or the weight of oedipal terrors, but rather by the shameful secret that I take refuge in the very burdens I claim to disdain? What if, like Natalie Barney, I am not a high-minded heiress who has dedicated her life, her fortune, and her considerable charms to the nurture of the arts and the selfless promotion of artists, but a talentless hack with a bottomless bank account and a need to control and dominate all who fall within my gravitational pull? What if, like me, I am not a gifted novelist who once took a wrong turn that has haunted him ever since, but a vaguely affable nonentity who has made all the right decisions for himself and his family except the one decision he needs to make—to once and for all kill off his obsolete, petrified self-image, and fully embrace the happiness that is his due?

That's a lot of what-ifs, but "what if" is a question, not an answer. We can ask a thousand what-ifs about ourselves and never be closer to the truth. What can "You must change your life" possibly mean in such circumstances? How can we know who we are and whether we are heading in the right direction if we can't even know whether to count ourselves among the living or the dead?

Guy de Maupassant's 1887 short story "The Horla" is not exactly a ghost story, but in many ways it answers to the prescription even better. It is, to be sure, one of the oddest stories of its sort ever written and, for me at least, beggars easy analysis. It's written in the form of the diary entries of an unnamed, well-to-do French bachelor over the course of three months. Out of the blue, he begins to experience anxiety attacks, undifferentiated fears, malaise, and nightmares. He dreams that someone is watching him, climbing onto his chest at night and trying to strangle him, to suck the life from his breath. Every morning, he finds his bedside water carafe mysteriously emptied. He finds relief in traveling, but all the symptoms recur even more strongly upon his return home. Gradually he becomes convinced that he is being stalked by an invisible being, the advance agent of a superior species that is destined to turn humankind into a slave race. The creature learns to dominate his thoughts and his will, and thereby prevents him from attempting another escape. Occasionally, he is able to detect physical evidence of its presence, such as the broken stem of a rose or a blurred image in the mirror, and he comes to believe that he can hear it whisper its own name: the Horla. In the end, he tries to kill it by locking it in his bedroom and setting fire to his house, but he comes to understand that it cannot be destroyed and that his only option for relief is, instead, to kill himself.

You can, of course, choose to interpret the story literally as an expression of the nineteenth-century discourse on the inroads being made by science into the realms of the unknown. Maupassant prepares us for such an interpretation with disquisitions on the inadequacy of government, religion, science, and occultism to explain and govern the natural world. There is so much that we do not know and cannot see, the theory goes, that it would be perfectly natural for a new, hitherto unsuspected species to rise to dominance as man once did. But this is a very one-dimensional way of reading a story that offers far more insight into psychology than into science.

The narrator naturally suspects at first that he is losing his mind, and it is only following a successful experiment with the carafe that he becomes convinced that he is dealing with an external force. But the experiment is convincing only if you really want to believe it; from start to finish, it remains perfectly plausible that the man is having a mental and emotional breakdown, and that every manifestation of apparently

supernatural agency is instead the projection of psychic turmoil. It makes far more sense to assume that the protagonist
has been rising from his bed, without waking, to empty the
carafe than that a malevolent, supernatural emanation has
been doing so. It becomes apparent that, although invisible
and endowed with mind-control abilities, the Horla is otherwise oddly humanlike—it reads books, carries flowers up
to its nose, has hands to strangle with and knees to crouch
upon, and can be startled by sudden, aggressive movement.
The narrator consistently refers to it as a person, not a thing.
If this were a twentieth-century story, there would be no
doubt whatsoever that the Horla is the narrator's embodied
neuroses and fears, and a projection of his own psyche. He
is, in effect, haunting himself. You could take it even further, if you liked, and make it a political tale of late-capitalist
degeneration—the bourgeois psyche devouring itself.

It might also be helpful to know that Maupassant wrote the
story while he was in the late stages of syphilis, enduring in-
creasing mental anguish, suffering episodes of paranoia, fear
of death, and persecution, and requiring constant solitude—
all symptoms shared by the narrator of "The Horla." Only
five years after writing the story, Maupassant tried to commit
suicide by slitting his own throat, and was thereafter confined to the asylum where he would die in 1893. It would be
no stretch of the imagination to interpret "The Horla" as a
self-portrait, but you hardly need to endure tertiary neu-
rosyphilis to feel that you are being haunted by a presence
that you cannot define yet closely resembles yourself in almost every particular. The intelligence that haunts the nar-

rator of Maupassant's story is the same as that which speaks
to Rilke from the ancient torso. It is his own ghost. It's no
coincidence that one original meaning of the verb "to haunt"
was "to be familiar with," and that it shares its root with the
noun "home." Home is always where the ghosts live.

We talk about being haunted by our memories, skeletons
in the closet, ghosts in the attic. I used to have a recurring
dream in which I suddenly remembered that, years earlier,
I had murdered my mother and concealed her body under
the floorboards. Although the dream begins only moments
before my secret is about to come to light, the memories—
memories of a life and a crime that never occurred—are fully
formed and available. Where did they come from? In real life
I did not murder my mother, but she did die in painful and
prolonged circumstances when I was of an age that I somehow
felt responsible for her distress and guilt for being sickened
and embarrassed by her illness, her rotting physicality, and
for wanting it all to simply go away. So again, it's hardly a
stretch to say that I am truly haunted, just like the narrator of
"The Horla," not by my mother's ghost—because I know that
"she" does not blame me, the child I was, for anything that
happened—but by the ghost of myself at that age. It is the ghost
of a boy stumbling about in the dark, his arms outstretched
and groping, his mind addled by drugs, liquor, and guilt,
without the slightest idea of where or who he is and with the
dawning sense that he may be alone in a universe of his own
devising. It is me and it is not me, and I haven't the slightest
idea of what he wants from me or how to lay his spirit to rest.
All I know is that he is out there and that he is fumbling for

a way to breach the barrier that separates the two of us. I can hear him late at night, when all is quiet, and sometimes he even speaks to me through the voice of my own children. Like all ghosts, he needs something that only the living, only I, can give him.

A person can be haunted by regret, but also, like Rilke, by anticipation. We're haunted not only by what happened but also by what didn't happen; not only by the dead but also by the living; not only by what we said but also by what we failed to say; not only by living fears but also by dead dreams; not only by the restless souls of others but also by our own.

But being haunted isn't inevitably a bad thing. To be haunted is to be accompanied. To be haunted is to be never alone. To be haunted is to have someone to talk to, to explain ourselves to, to offer us a new perspective on our circumstances. In *The Others*, the mother, played by Nicole Kidman, has no idea that she is dead or that her children are dead and that long ago she had killed them before turning the gun on herself. The creepy servants are in fact ghosts whose mission is to help her understand her real circumstances and who she is, so that she can go on with her existence without fear or confusion, and ultimately they succeed in doing so. That relief, of course, is what we all seek for ourselves.

In the same way, perhaps we shouldn't be afraid of the ghosts traveling all the roads we have not taken, all the possible lives that withered on the vine because we did not choose them, and consequently all the people we might have become and did not, and who startle us when we look in the mirror. They are not there to "haunt" us in the traditional sense—to frighten us, to scare us away, to fill us with regret, remorse, and sadness, to make us second-guess ourselves and the choices we have made. They are there to frequent us, to keep us company, to hold our hands and to guide us. If we allow ourselves to hear their voices—the voices of those people we never became, but could well have become—we may find that they are not so different from our own. Really, they are our own voices, all of them, as we will know if we still our breath long enough to listen to them.

Let us go back to Robert Frost's poem, in which, we recall, there are two roads. There is the road less traveled by, which is the one he takes, and the road not traveled. Frost describes them as "just as fair" as one another. He tells us that he chose the one over the other because "it was grassy and wanted wear," but then he concedes that "the passing there / Had worn them really about the same." In other words, there was very little to choose between them, and it is only in retrospect that he was able to conjure a justification for taking one over the other. Perhaps the road not taken ran perfectly parallel to the road less traveled by for miles and miles. Perhaps they diverged then crossed again farther along. Perhaps, as they emerged from the woods, the two roads merged and led all walkers to the same final destination.

Nevertheless, that choice made all the difference.

ACKNOWLEDGMENTS

The following people have all earned my sincere gratitude for a variety of reasons:

My wife, Judy Clain, who is my beloved advisor, guide, and companion in all things.

My sister Nancy Browner, my hero and inspiration.

My daughters, Sophie and Cora, who know why.

My publisher, editor, and friend Karen Rinaldi, who has put her faith in me time and again for reasons known only to her.

My agent, Gail Hochman, who has guided my career since before I knew I even had a career.

My dear friend Alice Quinn, who started it all and has kept the ball rolling ever since.

Kevin Larimer of *Poets & Writers* magazine, whose early support and enthusiasm were critical to this project.

My fearless and insightful early readers Jennifer Browner, Charlott Card, Barbara Clain, David Clain, Catherine Chermayeff, Shelley Sonenberg, and most especially Hertzie Clain.

And the generous friends who helped me crowd-source my research: Lefa Alksne, Jan Berman Wirth, Angus Burnett,

Lionel Cherruault, John Cooper, Amanda Dowd, Mark Ebner, Gabrielle Feldman, Sylvie Ferrando, Anne Frid de Vries, Elizabeth Gordon, Alon Gratch, Jane Greenbaum, Betsy Israel, Patrick Jackson, Darius James, Jodi Levy Collins, Karen Karbo, Anne Katzenbach, Liza Lagunoff, Niki Lambros, Susan Levine, Susan Lyne, Tom Maiello, Rue Matthiessen, Antonya Nelson, Andrea Nussinow, Lizzie Pickering, Jenifer Rabinowitz, Barbara Rathbone, James Rodewald, Victoria Rowan, Lia Samuel, Scott Sanders, Paul Schomer, Ira Silverberg, Bill Skutch, David Speciner, Ivan Stoler, Alla Zbinovsky, and Miriam Zyndorf.

REFERENCES AND READINGS

INTRODUCTION

Heraclitus. *Fragments*. Translated by Brooks Haxton. New York: Penguin Classics, 2003.

Robert Frost. *The Poetry of Robert Frost: The Collected Poems*. Edited by Edward Connery Lathem. New York: Henry Holt, 1979.

Jesse Browner. "Lives of the Civil Servants." *Poets & Writers*, August 31, 2012.

Milan Kundera. *The Unbearable Lightness of Being*. Translated by Michael Henry Heim. New York: Harper & Row, 1984.

Eric Naiman. "When Dickens Met Dostoevsky." *Times Literary Supplement*, April 10, 2013.

Adam Phillips. *Missing Out: In Praise of the Unlived Life*. New York: Farrar, Straus and Giroux, 2013.

Diderot et Falconet: Correspondence. Edited by H. Dieckmann and J. Secznec. Frankfurt: Vittorio Klostermann, 1959.

Edmund White. "Harold Brodkey." In *Mentors, Muses and Monsters*, edited by Elizabeth Benedict. New York: Free Press, 2009.

Scott Sherman. "The Idler: On Geoff Dyer." *The Nation*, May 9, 2011.

ON AMBITION

Henri Murger. *Bohemians of the Latin Quarter*. London: Vizetelly & Co., 1888.

Roger Shattuck. *The Banquet Years*. New York: Harcourt, Brace, 1958.

John Glassco. *Memoirs of Montparnasse*. New York: Oxford University Press, 1970.

René Daumal. *A Night of Serious Drinking*. Translated by David Coward and E. A. Lovatt. Boulder, CO: Shambhala, 1979

David Rattray. "Weekend with Ezra Pound." *The Nation*, November 16, 1957.

Marvine Howe. "David Rattray, 57, Poet and an Editor at Reader's Digest." *New York Times*, March 25, 1993.

"David Rattray reads from his translation of Artaud." YouTube video. Posted by "semiotexte." December 12, 2007. www.youtube.com/watch?v=vOlD2oqNdeo.

Homer. *The Odyssey*. Translated by Robert Fagles. New York: Viking, 1996.

J. Carruthers. "The Principles and Practices of Mentoring." In *The Return of the Mentor: Strategies for Workplace Learning*. Edited by Brian J. Caldwell and Earl M. A. Carter. London: Falmer Press, 1993.

Andy Roberts. "The Origins of the Term Mentor." *History of Education Society Bulletin*, no. 64 (November 1999): 313–29.

Todd Mitchell. "Career Wise." *Best's Review*, October 1, 2009. Archived copy available at www.thefreelibrary.com/Career+wise-a0209618625.

Jay McInerney. "Getting Your Novel Underway." *Writer's Digest*, March 11, 2008.

Betsy Sussler. "David Greig Rattray, 1936–1993." *Bomb*, no. 44 (Summer 1993).

David Rattray. *How I Became One of the Invisible*. New York: Semiotext(e), 1992.

Garett Caples. " 'Death Will Be My Final Lover': The Life of Alden Van Buskirk." *poetryfoundation.org*, http://www.poetryfoundation.org/article/244296

David Rattray interview with Ken Jordan. *Semiotext(e)*, December 1991.

ON LOVE

Donald Hall. *Life Work*. Boston: Beacon Press, 2003.

W. B. Yeats. "The Choice." In *The Collected Poems of W. B. Yeats*. Edited by Richard J. Finneran. New York: Scribner, 1996.

Rainer Maria Rilke. *Letters to a Young Poet*. Translated by Stephen Mitchell. New York: Vintage, 1986.

Andrew Romano. "The Beatles Succeeded Through Talent, Ambition, and a Lot of Arrogance." *The Daily Beast*, November 10, 2013, www.thedailybeast.com/articles/2013/11/10/the-beatles-succeeded-through-talent-ambition-and-a-lot-of-arrogance.html.

Scott Sherman. "The Idler: On Geoff Dyer." *The Nation*, May 9, 2011.

Liz Colville. "*Everything Happens Today* by Jesse Browner." *Bookforum*, October 25, 2011.

Anicius Boethius. *The Consolation of Philosophy*. Translated by Victor Watts. New York: Penguin Books, 2003.

André Aciman. "How Memoirists Mold the Truth." *New York Times Magazine*, April 7, 2013.

Bede. *A History of the English Church and People*. Translated by Leo Sherley-Price. New York: Penguin Books, 1955.

Jonathan Mahler. "The Coach Who Exploded." *New York Times Magazine*, November 6, 2013.

Kathryn Chetheovich. "Envy." *Granta*, no. 82 (Summer 2003).

Benjamin Anastas. *Too Good to Be True*. New York: Little A, 2012.

Joyce Carol Oates. "Notes on Writerly Influences." In *Mentors, Muses and Monsters*, edited by Elizabeth Benedict. New York: Free Press, 2009.

Dwight Garner. "A Collection of Characters, Beginning with the Author." *New York Times*, July 18, 2013.

Kathryn Schulz. "Don't Regret Regret." TED talk, November 2011. www.ted.com/talks/kathryn_schulz_don_t_regret_regret.

ON FREEDOM

Elena Ferrante. *Fragments: Elena Ferrante on Writing, Reading and Anonymity*. Translated by Ann Goldstein. Europa Editions, e-gift.

James Woods. "Women on the Verge." *The New Yorker*, January 21 2013.

Milan Kundera. *The Unbearable Lightness of Being*. Translated by Michael Henry Heim. New York: Harper & Row, 1984.

Ann Patchett. *This Is the Story of a Happy Marriage*. New York: Harper, 2013.

Rollo May. *The Courage to Create*. New York: Norton, 1975.

Larissa MacFarquhar. "Requiem for a Dream." *The New Yorker*, March 11, 2013.

Meghan O'Rourke. "The Recluse: Rescuing the Poet Jack Gilbert from Oblivion." *Slate*, May 9, 2005, www.slate.com/articles/news_and_politics/the_highbrow/2005/05/the_recluse.html.

Debbie Elliott. "Interview with Poet Jack Gilbert." *All Things Considered*. National Public Radio, April 30, 2006.

Sarah Fay. "Jack Gilbert (The Art of Poetry No. 91)." *The Paris Review*, no. 175 (Fall/Winter 2005).

Jack Gilbert. *Refusing Heaven*. New York: Alfred A. Knopf, 2012.

Suzanne Rodriguez. *Wild Heart: A Life—Natalie Clifford Barney's Journey from Victorian America to Belle Epoque Paris*. New York: Ecco, 2002.

Natalie Clifford Barney. *Adventures of the Mind*. Translated by John Spalding Gatton. New York University Press, 1992.

Natalie Clifford Barney. *Pensees d'une amazone*. Paris, Emile-Paul Freres, 1921.

Natalie Clifford Barney. *A Perilous Advantage: The Best of Natalie Clifford Barney*. Edited and translated by Anna Livia. Norwich, VT: New Victoria Publishers, 1992.

ON FULFILLMENT

Lewis Hyde. *The Gift*. New York: Random House, 1983.

Franz Kafka. *"The Metamorphosis," "A Hunger Artist," "In the Penal Colony," and Other Stories*. Translated by Ian Johnston. Arlington, VA: Richer Resources Publications, 2009.

Benjamin Nugent. *Elliott Smith and the Big Nothing*. Cambridge, MA: Da Capo Press, 2004.

Matthew Fritch. "Down on the Upside." *Magnet*, no. 46 (September/October 1998).

Liam Gowling. "Mr. Misery." *Spin*, December 2004.

Marcus Kagler. "Elliott Smith: Better Off Than Dead." *Under the Radar*, Spring 2003.

Matthieu Ricard. *Happiness: A Guide to Developing Life's Most Important Skill*. Translated by Jesse Browner. New York: Little, Brown, 2007.

Ernst Pawel. *The Nightmare of Reason: A Life of Franz Kafka*. New York: Farrar, Straus and Giroux, 1984.

Franz Kafka. *The Diaries, 1910–1923*. Edited by Max Brod. Translated by Joseph Kresh and Martin Greenberg with the cooperation of Hannah Arendt. New York: Schocken Books, 1976.

Adam Phillips. *Missing Out: In Praise of the Unlived Life*. New York: Farrar, Straus and Giroux, 2013.

ON WISDOM

Rainer Maria Rilke. *The Selected Poetry of Rainer Maria Rilke*. Translated by Stephen Mitchell. New York: Random House, 1989.

Guy de Maupassant. "The Horla" in *Selected Short Stories*. Translated by Roger Colet. London: Penguin Books, 1971.

Robert Frost. *The Poetry of Robert Frost: The Collected Poems*. Edited by Edward Connery Lathem. New York: Henry Holt, 1979.

Anthony Storr. *The Art of Psychotherapy*. New York: Routledge, 1990

Rosemary Gordon. *Dying and Creating: A Search for Meaning*. London: Karnac Books, 2000.

Marie-Louise von Franz. "The Process of Individuation." In *Man and His Symbols*, edited by Carl Jung. Garden City, NJ: Doubleday, 1964.

ABOUT THE AUTHOR

Jesse Browner lives in New York City.